ADVANCE PRAISE FOR *BE MORE PIRATE*

"Sam has created something that is timely and important. It is an idea that's going to explode."

—Will Hudson, founder and CEO of It's Nice That and Anyways

"If you're in an industry facing disruption, the challenges are huge and the practical solutions few and far between. *Be More Pirate* is a dynamic framework for taking charge of the change that's coming your way. Sam has made pirates relevant again."

—Adam Day-Lewin, creative director of Hearst Publishing and ex–creative director of Condé Nast

"*Be More Pirate* makes modern-day heroes of names lost in history. Sam has spotted something: that millennials are natural pirates in spirit, making their own way on the high seas. Put aside the cutlass-and-parrot pirates in the *Treasure Island* mold. The ones he is thinking of were the model for how to break the system and create radical change."

—Joy Lo Dico, *London Evening Standard*

"*Be More Pirate* is a timely kick up the backside for any organization that hasn't got to grips with the disruption that faces us all. But it's also an optimistic, practical, and purposeful rallying cry that a different way of organizing ourselves is possible. Who knew the rogues of the eighteenth century were going to be the role models we need for the twenty-first century."

—Stephen Woodford, CEO of the Advertising Association

T0089181

"Be More Pirate is a call to our better natures, our more inventive, imaginative selves to rouse up and remake the world. It's time for the rebels in us all to reemerge."

—Antony Mayfield, founder and CEO of Brilliant Noise

"A much-needed call for more radical intention at the top. *Be More Pirate* is more useful, memorable, and amusing than most leadership material I've seen, and I've pretty much seen the lot."

—Liam Black, CEO of Wavelength

"Be More Pirate is a brave, original, and inspiring concept."

—Syima Aslam, director and founder of Bradford Literature Festival

"Be More Pirate provides high-octane inspiration in the face of unprecedented disruption. Break open the rum and immerse yourself, because *Be More Pirate* is a holistic strategy for success in changing times."

—Sherilyn Shackell, founder and CEO of the Marketing Academy

BE MORE PIRATE

OR HOW TO TAKE ON THE WORLD AND WIN

SAM CONNIFF ALLENDE

ATRIA PAPERBACK

NEW YORK   LONDON   TORONTO   SYDNEY   NEW DELHI

ATRIA
PAPERBACK

An Imprint of Simon & Schuster, Inc.
1230 Avenue of the Americas
New York, NY 10020

Copyright © 2018 by Sam Conniff Allende
Previously published in 2018 by Touchstone, an imprint of Simon & Schuster
Originally published in Great Britain in 2018 by Portfolio. Portfolio is a publishing imprint in the Penguin Random House group of companies.

This Atria Paperback edition October 2021

ATRIA PAPERBACK and colophon are trademarks of Simon & Schuster, Inc.

For information about special discounts for bulk purchases, please contact Simon & Schuster Special Sales at 1-866-506-1949 or business@simonandschuster.com.

The Simon & Schuster Speakers Bureau can bring authors to your live event. For more information or to book an event, contact the Simon & Schuster Speakers Bureau at 1-866-248-3049 or visit our website at www.simonspeakers.com.

Manufactured in the United States of America

3   5   7   9   10   8   6   4   2

Library of Congress Cataloging-in-Publication Data

Names: Allende, Sam Conniff, author.
Title: Be more pirate : or how to take on the world and win /
by Sam Conniff Allende.
Description: New York : Touchstone, [2018] | Includes bibliographical references. |
Identifiers: LCCN 2018042151 (print) | LCCN 2018043411 (ebook) |
ISBN 9781982109622 (Ebook) | ISBN 9781982109615 (pbk.)
Subjects: LCSH: Change (Psychology) | Success. | Courage. | Pirates.
Classification: LCC BF637.C4 (ebook) | LCC BF637.C4 A46 2018 (print) |
DDC 650.1—dc23
LC record available at https://lccn.loc.gov_2018042151

ISBN 978-1-9821-0961-5
ISBN 978-1-9821-0962-2 (ebook)

For Scarlett, Frida, and Vivi

The average man will bristle if you say his father was dishonest, but he will brag a little if he discovers that his great-grandfather was a pirate.

—Bernard Williams

CONTENTS

CONTENTS

CTRL.ALT.DELETE
PIRATE

Part One

CTRL ALT DELETE
PIRATE

1. HERE BE DRAGONS

New Horizons, New Heroes

Three hundred years ago a small group of frustrated and underappreciated, mostly young professionals finally had enough of living in a society run badly by a self-interested and self-serving establishment. Disruption had become the constant backdrop to their lives as they faced ongoing uncertainty and mass redundancy in a world plagued by ideologically influenced international conflict. This generation felt entirely abandoned, and they were right. The odds were stacked high against them and in every single way, the rules of the day favored an elite few, and for the majority of people life was unclear, unfair, and unfulfilling.

Sound familiar?

Rather than simply voice their complaints, they chose instead to do something about the situation. No longer prepared to sit quietly and accept the bad deal on the table, they decided to break the rules and then remake the rules. Along the way, they came up with a new social code built on purposeful principles such as fair pay, fair say, social equality, freedom, and justice. And rum.

You see, the action these particular disenchanted professionals took was to turn pirate. Although such an extreme-sounding career change was arguably justifiable, these rebels, who emerged from both the Merchant and the Royal Navy, were soon denounced as "enemies of humanity" by the establishment they struck fear into, not only because of their unlawful buccaneering but also because of the radical and progressive ideas they represented.

These were the "Golden Age" pirates, and they created enough disruption at the edges of society and politics during this, the dawn of capitalism, to leave a legacy that has changed the way we live forever. Which is handy, because, some three centuries down the line, we're once again in need of inspiration about the best way to give the current establishment a metaphorical kick up the backside, to better tackle the world's looming crises.

Today we have a similarly self-interested political and business elite pressing the buttons of power, who for the most part show no sign of stepping up to the challenge in any meaningful sense. Rather than gracefully handing over a little more authority to the generations destined to live with their mistakes the longest, the folks who have already overcooked the future continue to run the show (a) in their own interests and (b) badly.

In their defense, it hasn't all been completely disastrous. From antibiotics to nanosurgery to the realization of the internet to lifting a billion people out of poverty to the Spice Girls, some of the progress in the late twentieth century truly demonstrated humankind at its best. But then we left the great fridge door of history open and everything started to go off. Today a multitude of futures await, most of them apocalyptic: environmental degradation, economic disintegration, unprecedented levels of human migration, or the rise of the robots—just take your pick.

In direct response to this turbulence, uncertainty, and the resulting emptiness many us face, much of society is afflicted by an epidemic of anxiety and a crisis of identity. Living costs are rising while real incomes are falling and the distribution of both wealth and opportunity grow more unequal than ever. Whole generations feel excluded from their own future. They are sick of being told "that's just the way things are" and that they're "naive" for expecting such basic amenities as decent housing or accessible health care or affordable higher education.

There's a lot of people we could blame for the mess we're in, but so far that's got us nowhere fast. What happens next is up to us; we each have to decide whether we're part of the problem or part of the solution, and when I say we, I mean you.

A lot of people might tell you not to worry, that technology will save us and everything will be okay in the end. But it's not true. No one is coming to save you. It's going to get worse before it gets better. There's an urgency in the air and a need for change. Today, if we want to improve this picture of our future, we have to do it ourselves. The only way out of this mess is a little less Instagram and a lot more action.

The upside to an age of uncertainty is that it is fertile ground for opportunity. Most of us are familiar with the feeling that if we could just get focused, come up with a plan, hustle a bit harder, and seize the opportunity, we could do good, if not great, things. There are smart people doing interesting things everywhere, but instead of being inspired by them, we find it easy to feel overwhelmed or intimidated.

So many successful people look more like superheroes than real-life characters whose steps you could realistically follow in. The typical role models that often get served up are well meant, but let's face it, they're also a little predictable. I want us to go further than the standard Stanford University dropouts with great teeth, quirky surnames, and heads full of world-changing technology. The thing is, every exciting unicorn galloping out of Silicon Valley leaves a lot of horse shit behind the scenes. I think we deserve more than the uberization of everything as our default universal future model of anything, and that's why I've looked to a different set of rebels, not just for inspiration but for practical ideas that anyone can take, adapt, and implement in order to change whatever it is that needs fixing, overhauling, or scrapping.

We're going to look back in time to the secrets of a unique set of pirates in order for you to navigate a more promising path for the future, one that sets you on the right track for the fortune you seek.

Whether you aspire to be a world-class change-maker or you'd just like a new career, whether you're trying to make your name, up your game, strike it rich, or strike a blow to the system, *Be More Pirate* will help you be more courageous, more effective, and more creative as we sail into the uncharted waters of the mid-twenty-first century.

Whether you're thinking about setting up your own business or trying to improve the one you're already in, whether your side hustle needs another side hustle, or if all you know is that you've got what it takes to be the next big thing, *Be More Pirate* will help you be more decisive, more powerful, and more purposeful in getting there.

Why are these Golden Age pirates the perfect role models

for anyone trying to make their mark against the odds we face today? Well, they didn't just break rules, they rewrote them. They didn't just reject society, they reinvented it. They didn't just tell tall tales, they told a story that shook the world. They didn't just challenge the status quo, they challenged everything, and once the dust had settled, their alternative society and strategies changed the world for good.

Yes, these are big claims. And yes, I'm going to back them up, and then some. Over the years, pirates have acquired a mythical status. They have been popularized and presented as pop-culture pastiches that don't resemble the true picture. *Be More Pirate* looks past these clichés and analyzes their innovations, organizational systems, and team structures that have become a global standard of good governance and their pioneering work on branding and reputation management, which predates the universal principles followed by best-in-class marketing and communications today. In the coming chapters, we'll explore which of the pirates' systems, beliefs, and attitudes will be valuable to anyone searching for treasure in these uncertain times.

We'll learn how a sense of purpose spurred the pirates forward and that, beneath the black flag, many also fought not only for booty but also for social change, justice, and freedom. We'll observe the economics, mechanics, and tactics that allowed pirates to take on the world, and explore how they designed a unique and dynamic system of principles to live by: the fluid but highly effective Pirate Code, which has had extraordinary influence on many twenty-first-century institutions and can now be harnessed individually by you. We'll learn the techniques of ground-breaking pirates of old like the "Pirate

King" Henry Avery, "Black" Bartholomew Roberts, and the legendary Anne Bonny, and compare them to their modern-day equivalents such as Elon Musk, Chance the Rapper, and Malala Yousafzai. These figureheads, new and old, made their own way and amassed vast influence (and often vast fortunes) to make a huge and reverberating dent in the world around them.

Forget everything you thought you knew about pirates Before we go any further, we need to address some concerns you might be having and walk a few myths off the plank (including plank walking, because the truth of the matter is that there really were no planks or any hapless victims being walked off them).

I'm guessing the word *pirate* makes you think of Johnny Depp as Captain Jack Sparrow, or maybe the Disney version of Captain Hook, a slightly camp pantomime villain complete with eye patch, parrot, and pieces of eight. Or perhaps you don't buy the "jolly pirate" concept at all, and you're thinking to yourself, "Hang on, weren't pirates actually complete and utter bastards who reveled in theft, torture, rape, and murder?" The short answer to that one is "no, not every one," though admittedly there were a few psychos among them.

But before we deal with the dark side, let me make it clear that we will be drawing our inspiration from a very specific type of pirate from a very specific period of history. This is not a book about Somali pirates, Chinese pirates, or Roman, Greek, Norse, or Barbary pirates nor is it about looters, raiders, corsairs, or wreckers, interesting though they all are. No, this book draws its inspiration from those who ruled the waves from around 1690 to 1725, the so-called Golden Age of Piracy, when a handful of what author Guy Anthony De Marco calls "rock star" pirates set the world alight with audacious rebelliousness and a clear commitment to ideals of justice and equality.[1] The likes of Henry Morgan, "Black" Sam Bellamy, and the fearsome Edward Teach, aka Blackbeard, were infamous the world over for standing firm in front of, sticking a middle finger up at, and totally outsmarting the powers that be. Pirates went head to head with the world's mightiest military forces, the enormous resources of the first state-backed multinational corporations, and the combined strength of the global superpowers of the day. And, for nearly forty years, they won.

For hundreds of years, the true and troublesome story of pirates has been rewritten by the establishment they threatened. They have been painted as "enemies of humanity," psychopaths utterly beyond the bounds of civilized behavior, in order to distract wider society from their potentially incendiary exploration of ideas such as universal suffrage, fair pay, and workers' rights. Gradually, over generations, as their reputation passed into myth, their stories were watered down and turned into caricatures for children's birthday parties. Until now, when pirates are hardly regarded as progressive role models, but some of what they achieved could and should be inspiration for our times. That they have been unfairly sidelined becomes clear from a simple online experiment. Try searching Amazon books for other historical groups who emerged in response to unjust aspects of society. Search "civil rights" and you'll find almost 100,000 robust academic results. "Suffragettes" returns a library of literature and support materials offering thorough analysis on the subject.

If we perform the same search for "pirates," however, the first title that comes up is *Pirates Love Underpants*, a children's book with an eye-patched, parrot-balancing, striped-breeches-wearing, treasure-holding, toothless grinning pirate captain on the cover. *Pirate Pete and His Smelly Feet* is next up, followed by more children's books and then some romantic fiction featuring dashing captains and swooning maidens. It takes a long time to get to any actual history books, and I'm guessing I'm one of the few people who has read all of them. These frivolous incarnations of pirates do the Golden Age of Piracy a massive disservice; the charge that pirates were nothing but chaos merchants needs to be addressed, because "agents of change" would be a more accurate term. I'm going to help you open your mind in order to see past your doubts and discover the truth about the tricks, tactics, and techniques used by pirates to create change in the world.

Black Flags

What might your reservations be at this stage? That I'm glossing over the gory truth of pirate history or massively indulging in moral relativism? If so, then good; these would be valid concerns to have.

First of all, let's cover off the baddest of the bad men because, yes, there were some downright bloodthirsty pirates like Captain Montbars the Exterminator, or Ned Lowe, whose most infamous moment of madness came when he captured a treasure-laden ship only to watch the jewels slung overboard by a brave member of the captured crew; Lowe's response was to cut his prisoner's lips off, fry them, and force feed them back into his victim's lipless mouth before single-handedly hacking the rest of his captives to death. It's pretty clear that the psycho-pirates were very psycho indeed. However, they lived in violent times where torture was common practice by the military and public execution was popular entertainment for the populace. Consequently the daily remit for casual horror could be huge. But none of the psychopathic pirates made bloody by their bloody time will be featured in this book. None of them holds a place in history for much other than terrible deeds. None of them was a champion of change or a figurehead of pirate in-novation.

In his smart and funny book *The Psychopath Test*, the smart and funny Jon Ronson explores what it means to be a ma-niac and discovers that at the turn of the twenty-first century the usual average-Joe-to-psycho ratio is about 1 in every 100 peo-ple.[2] He reveals that among CEOs in business the normal ratio is five times higher. From the statistics and stories I've found of pirate crews, captains, and the overall community, it would seem that had Ronson applied his psychopath test to the Golden Age of Piracy he'd have found the same higher-than-average psycho ratio among pirate captains as he found in CEOs.

Whether it's the business world today or the pirates' world three hundred years ago, most people, most of the time, broadly operate within the codes of conduct and culture of the day with a handful of wackos at the top giving everyone else a bad name. Unfortunately, the wackos are always with us, but we don't have to follow them and we're certainly not here to learn from them. So, having got the small selection of real nutters out of the way, let's consider the question: How mad and bad were the rest? Well, they were pirates, which some might see as a bad start, but piracy, defined as "theft at sea," is as old as civilization itself and has always involved at least the threat of violence. And that's the point. The majority of Golden Age pirates tried to create the impression of violence while actively trying to avoid conflict wherever possible. I know that sounds counterintuitive but hear me out: pirates were heavily motivated to steer clear of actual violence because it made sense financially. For pirates, there was a clear case—fear equals profit and violence equals cost.

As Peter Leeson, economist and author of the award-winning *The Invisible Hook: The Hidden Economics of Pirates*, puts it:

> Pirates used the Jolly Roger to enhance their profit through plunder. But it was the profit motive that led them to overtake victims in the least violent manner possible. By signaling pirates' identity to potential targets, the Jolly Roger prevented bloody battle that would needlessly injure or kill not only pirates, but also innocent merchant seamen. Ironically, then, the effect of the death head's symbolism was closer to a dove carrying an olive branch.[3]

To prove that this is business sense, not nonsense, let's look at their balance sheets. Pirates had close to zero resources at their disposal to repair a damaged ship or replenish supplies. Even minor damage or loss was life-threatening to a crew who'd be hanged on sight at the next port; they couldn't afford to stick around too long for a tire change. A reduction in their famed speed and agility was equally dangerous: a boat with a hole in it is not convincingly threatening or a good getaway vehicle.

And then there's the pirates' pioneering social insurance practices. A pirate who was injured in battle received a payout from the ship's common pot of money: 800 pieces of eight for a lost leg or 600 for a lost arm. Their compensation practice was not only a great recruitment tool and a prescient prediction of public policy and eventually human rights but also a very substantial financial reason for the company to avoid any damaging skirmish.

Another practice that proves that most pirates weren't out to cause unnecessary violence is their treatment of the captains of the ships they commandeered. Before seeking volunteers to join their crew, of which there were many, the pirates would interview the captured sailors about the behavior of their captain. Had he been the brutal sort so many of the pirates had experienced in the navy, or had he been fair? If the answer was that he'd been a tyrant, he might find himself marooned on a fast-disappearing sandbank in hundred-degree heat with only a pistol to comfort himself. Had he treated the men well, more often than not he'd find himself richly rewarded. This example of pirates imposing their principles of good management practice could be viewed as their showing consideration for the suffering of their former colleagues. Or their tendency for revenge. Or both. Okay, maybe you're gradually coming round to the idea that pirates weren't always the crude, bloodthirsty thugs they're portrayed as. Possibly you're starting to see that they had a pretty enlightened approach to their enterprise.

But what about the inescapable fact that they traded on terror? That's surely a bad thing, even back then on the high seas? Well, I would agree, but I think it's essential to remember two things: first, I'm judging pirates by the morals of their own times, not ours, and, second, we need to look at the intentions behind their actions. At the time of the Golden Age of Piracy, chimney sweeping and mining were common forms of employment for preschool children and the transatlantic slave trade was a respectable middle-class investment opportunity. The point is not even so much that they were brutal times with different standards (though they were), it's more that the self-declared good guys were abusing, stealing, and murdering. In fact, the pirates were only cast as the bad guys when they started standing up to the so-called good guys. Who were, indeed, pretty bad. For instance the infamous East India Company, the trading arm of the British government and one of the world's first household business names, routinely used murderous violence to strike "trade deals" as part of their government-and monarchy-sanctioned proto-colonial business operations.

As Nirad Chaudhuri, an Indian-Bengali-English writer on colonialism, said, "the line that separates robbery from piracy organized by respectable and legitimate governments has always been a very fine one."[4] During the Golden Age of Piracy, depending on the state of international relations, some ships would be sailing under a royal letter of marque (a formal license to operate as an armed militia, where violence, murder, and thievery were lawful as long as a cut of the booty got kicked back to the palace). This pirate-like pastime was officially called privateering. However, if things were quiet on the international conflict's front and there were no letters of marque on the scene, the very same endeavor was renamed piracy. One person's privateer is another person's pirate.

Her European enemies nicknamed Queen Elizabeth I of England the Pirate Queen for her liberal use of letters of marque and privateers. They allowed her to amass vast wealth, discreetly sink the odd enemy ship, and lay the foundations for the British empire, all while kick-starting the Golden Age of piratical dominance on the seas. The Pirate Queen's right-hand man in all this was Sir Francis Drake, still regarded as a national hero by the British but a hated figurehead of piracy by, erm, well, everyone else.

Throughout the seventeenth and eighteenth centuries, priorities and politics were in constant flux; the same activities conducted by the same men were encouraged and then outlawed over and over again. Legal, illegal, pirate, privateer, hero, hanged, rinse, repeat. However, there was one critical difference between these original privateers and pirates of the Golden Age and those who followed later—namely the duality of their intention. Golden Age pirates may have been thieves, but they were also incidental pioneers of social and political equality, fair pay, health insurance, workplace injury compensation schemes, and same-sex marriages, enshrined in the new rules of society that they wrote for themselves.

And it's here we begin to see the potential power for some contemporary professional rule breaking. Pirates didn't settle for the promise of change only to go undelivered; instead, they challenged, broke, and then rewrote the rules for others to follow in their footsteps. It's a radical and risky path to establish new principles, but as pirates prove, sometimes breaking the rules, and making the rules is just a matter of perspective.

The view from here might look like a moral mess, but the proof of the benefits of the pirates' social movement was obvious to observers at the time.

This is Colonel Benjamin Bennet, in an unbiased and objective assessment of the pirate situation, reporting to the British government's Council of Trade and Plantations in 1718, where he said:

"I fear they will soon multiply for so many are willing to joyn with them when taken. . . ." The prospect of plunder and ready money, the food and the drink, the camaraderie, the democracy, equality, and justice, and the promise of care for the injured—all of these must have been appealing.

Colonel Bennet's voice is an official one with no agenda or empathy on behalf of the pirate cause. He was a military officer talking to an arm of government via formal channels, not an ancient "pyrate" justifying his crimes under a romantic banner. He had no reason to embellish the pirates' appeal which was already far too clear to him. The appeal of the pirate's new social contract had already begun to threaten the order of an outdated establishment.

The power of the unproven promise of the pirates' new society "for the many, not the few" is a timely reminder of the fragile impermanence of our own democracy and the risks we run if it is taken for granted. I know that citing democratic principles alongside Golden Age pirates might seem like a big leap, but I'm not alone in making the link, and it's a link we might learn from.

The host of the brilliant and scene-setting Pirate History Podcast, Matt Albers, tells an epic tale of the Golden Age pirates in beautiful detail across weekly episodes like this:

> It would be difficult to say that pirates began the first democracies since ancient times, but it wouldn't be totally out of the question to say they influenced [them] . . . and this was a very grave threat to the old empires. A group of rough and uncouth men, in a very couth age, decided that they were going to disregard the old order and try and start something where everybody had a voice. This was a threat to everybody in Europe. . . . They knew what a threat they [Golden-Age pirates] represented and they had to do everything they could to make sure that nobody ever in the New World would think like that again. Only about fifty years later there was a group of very genteel men in North America who had very similar leanings.[6]

To Matt and me, it would appear self-evident that pirates played a real role in both the formation and the fight for US identity, democracy, and independence, and it's this role of the rule breaker, in defense of democracy, which might just be another reason to reconsider their status from rogues to role models.

The Golden Age pirates' intentions are what challenged and terrified the official powers, and it's the disruptive effect of their promise of a progressive alternative to the established and unfair order that makes them worth learning from now.

Having established that a part of pirate history could provide advantageous yet underexplored inspiration for the world we face, we're nearly ready to set sail. In the next chapter, we'll Ctrl.Alt.Delete pirate history for good as we explore the pirates' innovative ideas and practices that can be valuable to those of you seeking treasure in these uncertain times.

In Part Two you'll learn how to be more pirate yourself and carve your own success by following their five simple stages of change. In researching and exploring the pirates, I've identified five key methods that they practiced, and developed a framework for you to be able to use them, too. These fundamental stages that underpin a pirate mind-set for creating change are:

1. Rebel—Draw strength by standing up to the status quo.
2. Rewrite—Bend, break, but most important rewrite the rules.
3. Reorganize—Collaborate to achieve scale rather than growth.
4. Redistribute—Fight for fairness, share power, and make an enemy of exploitation.
5. Retell—Weaponize your story, then tell the hell out of it.

The pirates questioned and challenged the established order, rebelled against the status quo, and then rewrote the rules. They came up with better alternative ideas and formed powerful communities of people who wanted to reorganize themselves in a new society. In these pioneering groups, the pirates made a point of fighting for fairness and inclusion. As they did this, they weaponized the art of storytelling and anticipated the idea of branding, crafting killer stories about themselves that helped magnify their reputation and establish their legacy. Of course they did all this alongside the rum, plunder, and looting you're more familiar with, but it's these five techniques that will be your basis for creating a *Be More Pirate* state of mind. In each of the five chapters that explore these behaviors we will keep checking in with the very best examples and achievements of groundbreaking pirates like Ben Hornigold, "Black" Bartholomew Roberts, and Mary Read, and inspirational modern-day pirates like Banksy, the Wu-Tang Clan, and Blockchain. Drawing on a mixture of pioneers old and new, you'll understand what it means to be more pirate and be shown how to adopt a piratical approach of your own. Takeaway sections at the end of each of these chapters will help you to think about what being more pirate might look like to you and how you can start to be more pirate in different areas of your life.

In order to help you apply these learnings to your life, Part Three will focus on the Pirate Code, the famous but misunderstood rules that governed each pirate enterprise. We'll look at how these codes helped the pirates establish their purpose, priorities, and principles and how you can harness their exact structure to build your own Pirate Code 2.0, a bespoke manifesto and mechanism to set you up for the success you deserve in the twenty-first century. Soon you will have an arsenal of surprising and invigorating pirate stories, you'll be armed with cunning pirate tricks and tactics to turn your ideas into action, and you'll know how to put more meaning into your mischief.

Be More Pirate will help you realize your inner ambitions and overcome your fears, make you more ruthless at bringing your ideas to life, and give you the confidence to fly your own flag and stand up for what you believe in. As we start to approach the end of the Information Age, the future is uncertain and nobody knows what's over the horizon. But it is certain that what you stand for will count more than ever, and who you stand up to will come to define you.

As we sail into the uncharted waters of the twenty-first century, where the odds once again favor the few, we need to take change upon ourselves and follow in the footsteps of pirate pioneers who took on their broken systems and fought for fairness as well as fortune, and changed our world by breaking and remaking the rules.

I know that for some of you embarking on a course of rule breaking might sound a disconcerting way to get things done, but consider this: great rule breakers are often like great painters, rarely appreciated for their art in the moment. How many statues are out there of people who were just following orders? History tells us time and again that progress depends on the rule breakers. And here we are again, living in historic times when the hour is likely to be upon us all when we have to decide if it's the right thing to do, to do the opposite of what we're told.

It's time to take courage. With those ideas of yours, that phone by your side, and this book in your hands, you have all that you need at your fingertips. So forget your preconceptions of pirates and have no fear about what's to come. If you're going to reinvent your future, it won't be by doing what you're told but by rewriting your own rules and being more pirate.

2. ENEMIES OF HUMANITY

There Are Pirates, and There Are Golden Age Pirates

To reap the many benefits of being more pirate, first you need to know more pirate. The true nature of the mischief and disruption they caused was deliberately distorted by those it threatened most. It's time to uncover their hidden history so you can use it to your advantage. It's time to explore the Golden Age pirates' real achievements so that you can follow in their footsteps and create similar change in your world.

If we are going to understand how these pirates reshaped their world, we first need to understand how their world shaped them. This exceptional bunch of men and women didn't spring from nowhere; they were products of their turbulent times and they were defined by what they fought for and stood against.

The Golden Age of Piracy is broadly understood to be the time between 1690 and 1725, with a particularly intense phase occurring in the 1710s that culminated in the creation of the Republic of Pirates on the Caribbean island of Nassau, where around 1,500 pirates were involved in a pioneering experiment in democracy that some argue was more participatory and representative than anywhere else on earth. In Nassau, right at the geographical epicenter of the slave trade, black people lived in freedom alongside all other colors with broadly equal rights. Nearly eighty years before the French Revolution demanded *liberté, égalité,* and *fraternité*, before Thomas Paine wrote his book *The Rights of Man* and Mary Wollstonecraft wrote *A Vindication of the Rights of Woman*, men and women, rich and poor, had a more equal say and enjoyed more equal rights than any other society in the world at the time. Golden Age pirates were not just individualistic fighters with a reputation for violence, out to get rich quick (although they were certainly this as well); they were also pioneers of collective action and social, political, racial, and almost every other kind of equality. The Golden Age of Piracy arose in response to a series of monumental man-made clusterfucks that came to define the early 1700s. The previous century had seen the world's empires binge on war like we do on box sets. Years of episodic conflicts created interconnected wars so long and complicated they killed, outlasted, or confused to death anyone who'd been around when they had begun.

To give you a fast flavor of the intermingling mess of all these melees, here are the top international battles that occurred in the buildup to the Golden Age of Piracy:

1. Dutch-Portuguese War—England and Holland vs. Portugal. Round one: ding ding.
2. Anglo-Spanish War—England vs. Spain. For England, for glory, for the first of many.
3. Anglo-French War—England vs. France. For good balance.
4. The Portuguese Restoration War—England, France, and Portugal vs. Spain. Just to mix it up a bit.
5. First Anglo-Dutch War—England vs. Holland. The clue is in the name.

6. Second Anglo-Spanish War—England vs. Spain. Again.
7. Second Anglo-Dutch War—England vs. France and Holland. Because one is never enough.
8. Anglo-Siamese War—England vs. Siam, a threat more than a full war, to teach poor old Siam a lesson for forcing the East India Company to close a factory.
9. The Third Anglo-Dutch War—England vs. Holland. Third time lucky, for the Dutch.
10. The Franco-Dutch War—England and France vs. Holland, Spain, Norway, Denmark, and the Holy Roman Empire. Forgive me, Father, for I have lost count of all these wars.
11. The Nine Years War—England, Holland, Spain, and the Holy Roman Empire (all the guys back together again as if all the above never happened) vs France. Of course.

And right in the middle of all that—because eleven international conflicts in a hundred years just wasn't enough for the bloodthirsty Brits—England fought a major war with itself, in three parts.

There was nothing civil about the English Civil War. A greater percentage of the country's male population perished in this domestic conflict than during the Second World War. Quite frankly, it's a mystery how there was anyone left to fight all the other wars taking place. What's less mysterious is why a life of bloody violence, conflict, and attacking Spain (or was that France?) might have seemed relatively normal by the turn of the eighteenth century. This culture of conflict and the inter-linking political and theological puzzles that came alongside each alliance created the conditions in which the pirates could thrive.

The Spanish War of Succession from 1710 to 1716 further developed the rise of the final and most famous and influential stage of the Golden Age of Piracy, not least because the end of the war meant nearly two-thirds of the enormous Royal Navy was now redundant. The scale of redundancy these career sailors faced forced them to seek new alternative employment, much as mass automation will force thousands, if not millions, of people to find new jobs in the next ten years.

Unlike today's taxi drivers, retail assistants, office clerks, call-center staff, and pizza delivery guys, all of whom might soon be given the chop by a robot hand, the sailors of the seventeenth century were fortunate enough to have already learned a trade they could utilize in a new self-employed format. They were experts in sailing, fighting, and stealing; they were well schooled in ambiguous morals and fluctuating allegiances, and after years of always exploitative and sometimes brutal working conditions, they were ready for a career change. They were precariously open minded to the promise of pirates who were offering not only wealth but also the chance of fair pay, fair treatment, and the opportunity to give the self-serving system a cutlass-sharp poke in the eye.

And what did they have to lose? The political leaders of the time were conspicuously interested in preserving their own power rather than trying to empower those they led. The ruling class was made up of international elites who were not averse to reinventing democracies, theocracies, and any other -ocracy they could lay their creepy gloved hands on if it gained them a scrap of advantage in what seemed to be a neverending fight for dominance. Generations had lived and died in back-and-forth fights between ideologies, where yesterday's heroes were tomorrow's villains. And, as we will soon be asking ourselves, what is a huge diaspora of despondent and redundant workers seeking meaning but without opportunity meant to do with itself?

The times were gloomy and people were anxious and exhausted. The only new opportunity promising adventure and financial reward was, quite literally, off the chart and very far from home. With the world powers of the time in decline, all eyes were on the wealth of the "New World." (Though, of course, the New World wasn't so new for the sophisticated Inca, Aztec, and Mayan populations whose millennia of civilization were set to be nonchalantly annihilated as a by-product of being "discovered.")

The Spanish empire was just about clinging on to its global choke hold, thanks to the unprecedented wealth it had stolen from territories in what is now Mexico and Peru using a lethal cocktail of bribes, lies, germs, guns, and God. As mankind took its formative steps in state-sanctioned corporate asset-stripping of the world's natural resources, the Spanish created the legendary pieces-of-eight system, primarily as a way of improving the stackable ship-homeability of their stolen silver and gold. A legendary emblem of pirate obsession was born.

All the Spanish Empire needed to do to thrive was subdue the natives with the blunt end of their Christian mercy, talk them out of their own heritage, steal their riches, and get safely back to Europe in their state-of-the-art, purpose-built transatlantic treasure-stealing fleets.

In turn, all the pirates had to do to thrive was be smart enough and fast enough to resteal the plunder of the world's foremost superpower right out from under their mustaches without getting hanged. This is what they set out to do, but when there are only about 1,500 on your team and you're taking on a sovereign nation, its empire, and its armada, you'd better bring your A game. (Or in this instance, your P game.) To succeed against odds like that, the pirates had to rely on techniques that would give them a competitive advantage. Namely, a fearsome reputation, applied imagination, creative strategy, a responsive network, a shared motivation for success, and a defining set of values and principles.

Pirates vs. Civilization Match Report

To bring home the case for pirates as rebels who make good role models, we're going to look more closely at how they operated and at the culture they created. We're going head-to-head as we put their innovations in the areas of fair pay, organizational structures, and equality to the test with the rest of civilization.

Pre-match prediction: an easy win for the pirates. They got more done in thirty years or so than most of us do in a lifetime. (Although to be fair, if you were a pirate in the Golden Age, thirty years probably *was* your expected lifetime.)

No Prey, No Pay in the Fight for Fairness

One of the pirates' earliest innovations, which is mentioned in historical records as far back as the 1690s, was the concept of a fair ratio of pay among crew members. Aboard a pirate ship, the captain and quartermaster took three or four shares of any loot, other essential or high-risk roles such as doctors and gunners received two shares, and all the other crew received one share, right down to the cabin boy.

It's not hard to imagine why the fair shares would have been a top priority for men fleeing the naval life. The navies, both merchant and royal, paid their crews very little, if they paid them at all. Wages were often late or less than the sum promised and sailors received no written contract on signing up. Some of them weren't even there voluntarily. Press-ganging, when men were either knocked unconscious or drugged and dragged aboard to work, was common. All too often, sailors in the navy were closer to indentured laborers than anything else.

Compare the pirates' fair and open systems with our current economic climate and rules on pay ratios and you'll start to get an immediate sense of just how radical the pirates really were. In the wake of the 2008–2009 financial collapse, commentators and critics from all over the world cited the enormous and unchecked gulf between the highest and lowest wages within certain businesses as a contributory factor to near economic Armageddon. Ahead of the collapse, in 2002 the ratio of CEO pay to the average salary stood at 384 to 1, its all-time high.[1] The creation of a fair pay ratio has been much discussed but rarely tested within mainstream business, except some Scandinavian countries (who else?) that have passed policies to limit CEO pay by linking it to the average workforce salary. This is already standard practice around the world within social enterprises (whose members run their businesses not for the profit of their shareholders but for a defined social good), where a 1 to 10 ratio is seen as a healthy scale between the lowest paid employee and the highest paid. That said, even this generous ratio results in much greater discrepancy between earnings than the one the pirates used.

Pirates 1–Civilization 0

At the time, the pirates' policy on fair pay ratios was revolutionary and had the far less fair but very well-paid powers that be shaking in their boots. Today, it's still way ahead of anything that contemporary organizations have managed to implement.

Checks and Balances, Protect What's Precious

Nonhierarchical structures were even more fundamental to the pirates' mission than the concept of fair pay. Around the 1680s the pirates came up with a robust system of checks and balances by elevating the existing seafaring role of quartermaster to the same status as captain. This simple but sophisticated move effectively created a two-house system, a nonexecutive, or a second umpire. The captain remained responsible for strategy while the quartermaster was fully responsible for culture and the way the ship was run on a day-to-day basis, as well as representing the voice of the crew.

Naval captains had a deservedly bad reputation. They were virtual dictators on board and operated without fear of rebuke by their superiors back on land. Many used brutal corporal punishment to keep order. As a result, they were often hated by their crews, who were only too keen to jump at the offer of a little less medieval way of life. The promotion of the quartermaster to balance a captain was a simple but sophisticated move to protect against any return to an abuse of power.

On this score, the pirates were not so much pioneering as embodying the spirit of the times. The English had been killing themselves, literally, over this point throughout the trilogy of the English Civil War until the 1689 Bill of Rights institutionalized formal powers of a second house of government in a move soon followed by the US, then replicated in most democracies. Soon after, the Bank of England Act of 1694 created the first effective "board" and began a similar dual executive system of checks and balances that can now be found the world over in nearly all organizations from charity to big business.

Pirates 2–Civilization 0

The pirates were only a few years in front of the rest of civilization on this one, but they still managed to peacefully implement and sustain an idea that mainstream society had to have a long and bloody fight with itself to come up with. As the pirates joined working-class heroes like the Levellers who had gone before them, their practices pioneered a new degree of expectation for universal working conditions.

One Pirate One Vote: More Participative Than Pericles

Surviving records from the 1690s onward illustrate that all members of pirate crews were given a say and a vote. That's everyone, including women (yes, there were a few) and nonwhites.

Universal suffrage, like dual governance and fair pay,

was a response to the brutal experiences many had suffered at the hand of dictatorial captains in the Royal and Merchant navies. But it's one thing to decide that the leadership should be a little less savage and quite another to shift the power totally by giving every single member of the crew a vote on major decisions.

It wasn't until 1928, some 240 years after the pirates had embraced the concept, that women gained the vote in the UK and universal suffrage was achieved. In the States, women gained the vote a little earlier (in 1920), but for nonwhite citizens the story was more complex. Despite an 1870 amendment to the Constitution that forbade any withholding of the vote on the grounds of race, the fight for fair and equal voting rights wasn't won until the 1950s.

Pirates 3–Civilization 0

Collective decision-making was a radical act, but a system that included female and non-white voices was revolutionary, and the first major upgrade to classic Athenian democracy in which only a third of society (all the white men, of course) had the vote.

Payouts and Peg Legs, No Pirate Left Behind

So I asked you to unlearn all you knew about pirates, but this is where I have to admit there is some truth to the stereotypical peg-legged and eye-patched pastiche. Piracy was a dangerous line of work; violence was commonplace, and one bad injury could mean the end of your career. In either navy, a mortal wound would have been considered bad luck and a hazard of the workplace. An unlucky ordinary sailor could become a swivel-eyed peg-legged drunk begging for change outside a rowdy tavern before he could say Billy Bones, but records show that Golden Age pirates routinely set aside a portion of everything they stole to serve as compensation when comrades were wounded. Payments included the aforementioned 800 pieces of eight for a lost leg through to 100 for a lost eye. Injured pirates were often even given the option to stay aboard a boat and continue contributing to the community by taking on a new role as cook or something else more suited to their new situation.

Two hundred years later the UK became the first developed economy to pass workplace compensation into law, due largely to the fact that it was the first fully industrial economy. Most major economies and democracies followed suit over the following century until social insurance was eventually recognized within the Universal Declaration of Human Rights in 1948.

Pirates 4–Civilization 0

There's a pattern emerging here, isn't there? Pirates come up with a great idea that the establishment tries to dismiss but which then becomes so popular among the people that eventually said establishment has no choice but to embrace it, and then pretend it was their idea. The pirates' ideas can be more innovative because they start on the edges, and through being well tested, they evolve to become popular and end up influencing the mainstream. These stages of change are something we'll build upon later in Part Two.

Seventeenth-Century Cocktail, Anyone?

Cocktails? You never mentioned cocktails! Well, yes. The pirates invented the cocktail way back in the 1560s. Sir Francis Drake, the grandfather of the Golden Age of Piracy, is known to have developed the first blended alcoholic beverage mixed with juice, sweeteners, and flavoring.

Drake's proto-cocktail was known as El Draque (The Dragon) after the Spanish nickname for Drake, the Englishman they most loved to hate. An El Draque included lime juice (for scurvy), rum (for reward), sugar (for energy), and a certain type of tree bark (for "medicinal" qualities). It's unlikely it was served over ice, but nonetheless it doesn't sound altogether bad (or unlike a mojito, just without the ice).

It took the nonpirate world nearly three hundred years to wake up to the magic of cocktails. The first recorded cocktail was the Old Fashioned, which made its appearance in 1860 in New York's high society circles. Cocktail parties quickly became all the rage, and the very first cocktail list was published as *How to Mix Drinks, or, The Bon-Vivant's Companion* in 1862.

Pirates 5–Civilization 0

Conclusion: It's a landslide victory for the pirates!

How you doing? I know it's a lot to take in. Previously, pirates were borderline comedy children's characters with a slightly shady past, and now look! The world's greatest innovators of social justice! Who knew?

Just for the record, it's highly unlikely that the pirates were the conscious architects of all this innovation; and it's important to remember this before we get carried away rebalancing their reputation. The pirates weren't secret sweeties blessed with lovely liberal values actively designing new social structures for the benefit of all of humanity. They were trying to fix the problems they saw in front of them, make their lives better, and let's not forget, amass great fortunes by aiming to steal other people's great stolen fortunes. They broke old rules and made new ones, and in the process came up with some prescient and progressive ideas by default.

But even if they were just out to change their world rather than *the* world, their record is impressive. Rarely has the world seen such an intense period of innovation, imagination, and achievement, or has such a lasting positive impact been created by so few. World War II, with all its radars, jet engines, and atomic bombs, could be comparable for productivity. Or maybe the turn of the nineteenth century, when you couldn't move for stepping on a lightbulb, some radium, or a telephone. Perhaps the first few decades of Silicon Valley, when frighteningly prolific nerds in awful sweaters created technology that would exponentially speed up human evolution, is up there, too. These are all moments when humankind quickened its step and produced huge growth spurts of thought that compounded imagination.

In each of these ages of advancement, the protagonists were products of their environment. The pirates had been pushed to the edges of society and the fringes of capitalism. And there in the shadows, outside society's gaze, beyond the rules, they were free to innovate and create their own methods. Being unconstrained by the way things *should be* allowed the pirates to experiment with the way things *could be*.

Brave New Worlds

Whenever new worlds are discovered, whether these worlds are what we now call North, Central, or South America or the vast digital new world, competition tends to arise between state-backed players (who seek to establish order) and those we call pirates (who seize treasure and opportunity).

Rather than write this off as the age-old battle of bad vs. good, it's possible to see this competitive relationship as one of creative evolution. Both sides represent a different approach to progress and ultimately help drive their opponent forward faster. Whether it's Apple and Microsoft, Jay Z and Kanye, or even Woody and Buzz, rivalry can play a positive role in the development of ideas as two competitors can achieve more, go further, and act braver through conflict than they might have done through cooperation. Each learns from the other's successes as much as their failings.

We've touched on how the stratified world of the establishment pushed the pirates to search for an alternative way of life which resulted in the creation of a progressive proto-democratic republic in the Bahamas. But the establishment also learned a great deal from the pirates and were driven to innovate technology, weapons, strategy, and even the social welfare of ordinary sailors as a result of the pirates' actions.

In *The Pirate Organization: Lessons from the Fringes of Capitalism*, economists Rodolphe Durand and Jean-Philippe Vergne explain that "the pirate organization is the necessary counterpart to capitalism . . . [and] determines the pace of capitalistic evolution."[2] They argue that capitalism creates normal ways to generate scale and industry, and that pirates force innovation, invention, and alternative methods of value creation. They conclude that the role of the pirate organization in exploring and understanding new worlds has always been essential, but it's also often been overlooked.

It's not hard to see how piracy has played this role and improved many inventions we all love. Apple gave the world iTunes because it was responding to music piracy, not because the music industry itself was actively looking for a new way to present music. Netflix defined the future of video with on-demand subscription models not because of a failed attempt at a partnership with Blockbuster but in response to early file-sharing pirates. In any industry, when a new territory is created, the threat of pirates drives forward the establishment's endeavors until the establishment is eventually overtaken. The threat of piracy is behind the truism that you have to innovate faster than others can imitate.

It is the piratical mind-set, methods, and achievements that drive change in all areas of society and always have. As Durand and Vergne put it:

> The pirate organization breaks the existing codes and creates new ones, which will later be reappropriated by legitimate governments and organizations. . . . This explains why the Pentagon and Microsoft track hackers in cyberspace to offer them a job or why pirate Francis Drake became a corsair before being knighted by the Queen of England. (p. 153)

Piracy is still on the whole regarded by the establishment as a bad thing even while it scrambles to adopt the successful innovations pirates created. It's safe to say that the positive output of the relationship with pirates is widely misunderstood in our day and age. Elon Musk, CEO of Tesla, SolarCity, and SpaceX, is one of the few mainstream business figureheads with a proactive plan to deal with piracy, even if at first it seems a counter-intuitive one. As Musk explained in an interview with Chris Anderson at *Wired*: "We have essentially no patents in SpaceX. Our primary long-term competition is in China. If we published patents, it would be farcical, because the Chinese would just use them as a recipe book."[3] Elon Musk's insightful understanding of how pirates work may just be because he's such a pirate paragon himself, but more on him and how he might fit the definition of a modern pirate later.

Pirate State of Mind

Now that you know more about the kind of revolutionary changes the Golden Age pirates were able to initiate—from inventing the cocktail to surprisingly progressive workplace culture and pay—any of your old preconceptions about pirates should have been consigned to the deep. Hopefully your mind is cooking up ideas and questions about how you can use pirate innovations to challenge and change your own environment. Just before we move into the specific strategies you can adopt, here is how we're defining pirates and what it means to be more pirate.

- Pirates challenge the establishment's authority and ownership of new ideas.
- Pirates innovate at the margins, free from the order of the ordinary.
- Pirates incubate their ideas in an intensive open-space environment.
- Pirates have a dual focus: fortune, then fairness.
- Pirates' acute focus on micro needs inadvertently creates macro solutions.
- Pirates tell their story at scale through their use of subversive tactics.
- Eat. Sleep. Pirate. Repeat.

Essentially, pirates trouble the edges of society and make enough shock waves to influence the middle ground. Trouble is their tool, although within a *Be More Pirate* state of mind, it's more accurate to call it good trouble.

The concept of "good trouble" is, for me, the absolute core of what it means to be more pirate. The term was coined by legendary civil rights activist and campaigner John Lewis, a US congressman. He has been using this term for years, drawing on his own experience that dates back to a famous bridge in Selma at the height of the civil rights movement in America. As a term, good trouble went viral in June 2016 when he staged a sit-in on the floor of the US House of Representatives, calling for change to the laws that govern gun sales in the wake of the Orlando nightclub shooting in which fifty people were killed. A couple of months later he gave a commencement speech to the graduating students of the Massachusetts College of Liberal Arts in which he urged them:

> Go out there, get in the way, get in trouble. Good trouble, necessary trouble, and make some noise. Our country needs you now more than ever before. When you see something that is not right, not fair, not just, you have a moral obligation, a mission, and a mandate to do something about it. Stand up, speak up, and speak out. Be brave. Be bold. Be courageous. . . . And never, ever let anything get you down.[4]

Being a troublemaker, even a good troublemaker, doesn't automatically make you a pirate, but I really believe that you can't be a pirate without the intention of making some good trouble.

Remember, pirates didn't set out to change the world, they just wanted to change their world. Pirates didn't intend to push forward democracy, they just wanted to make their own decisions. Pirates didn't mean to advance social policy, they just wanted to be treated fairly. Sometimes imagination compounds, and good ideas that are formed at the edges find their way to the center and change everything. They didn't just cause trouble, they caused good trouble.

For thirty years I've sailed the seas and I never seen good come o' goodness yet. Him as strikes first is my fancy; dead men don't bite; them's my views—amen, so be it.

—Israel Hands

If you want to be more pirate in life, then take a moment for reflection here. I've run Be More Pirate workshops all over the world with all sorts of teams, from students to senior executives, and there are a couple of challenges we use during the sessions that have been very successful for others. I want to share one of them here.

It's worth setting this up now, as I'm going to include some of the challenges that have had the most profound impact for people in my workshops at the end of some of the chapters.

I've left a page by each challenge for you to make notes, partly because I love the idea of this book becoming yours, and partly because giving yourself a few minutes to reflect when absorbing new information dramatically improves your relationship with, and your ability to benefit from, what you've learned.

And because while writing notes on your phone is easier, we both know you'll get distracted.

The Golden Age pirates took on the challenges of their time, and the solutions they created for their world then changed *the* world. The same is true of the more modern pirates we're going to look at, and the same is true of you. If you really want to take on the task of creating meaningful and lasting change, you need to make sure you know what gets in your way before you begin.

So, the challenge I invite you to consider upon before we embark on the rest of the book is:

What really holds you back in life?

Invest a few minutes and aim to come up with between five and fifteen points.

The things that hold you back could be your own habits, the self-sabotaging acts you semisubconsciously make every day, the boxes you let others put you in, or just the stuff you sometimes say to put yourself down. They could be things you let other people get away with, that bad habit you just don't ever get around to breaking, or something else. All that matters, if you're going to do this, is that you're really honest with yourself. Identifying honestly what truly gets in your way is going to make rebelling against it much easier later on.

Then if you have time, in the workshops what we'd do is take one more minute to look up and down the list and choose the one thing you do that holds you back the most; then put a cross through it.

One by one, in order of worst to least bad, put a slow, steady, and deliberate cross through each and every other one of those little pains in the ass. X marks the spot, so let them all die right there on the page.

Feel no guilt as you cross out the things that drive you mad or hold you back. The point is to identify the barriers you face. By the time you've finished this book, bad habits and self-doubt will be a distant memory, leaving you no option but success.

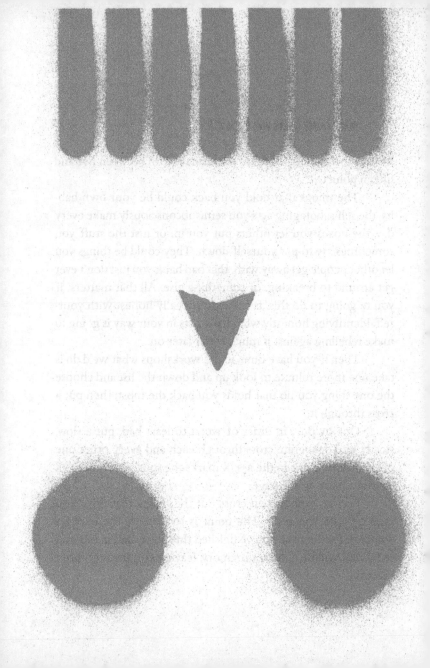

3. PIRATE CHRONICLES

Before we dive into the five stages of change that will help you to be more pirate, I'd like to present a timeline of the very best dates in pirate history. I know timelines are boring with a capital T, but this one is full of intriguing pirate facts that will also give context to your understanding of the Golden Age of Piracy, how they came about and how they changed the world. Though interesting, it's not mandatory reading, so please feel free to skip it if you're not up for a pirate nerd-off.

1000
(ROUGHLY)
Leif Erikson the Viking is the first European to "discover" the Americas after being blown off course on his Viking way to Greenland.

1492
Christopher Columbus "discovers" America and introduces its inhabitants to industrial-scale slavery, torture, forced labor, disease, and near extinction.

1533

Queen Elizabeth I is born to Henry VIII and Anne Boleyn. She was later nicknamed the Pirate Queen by the Pope and the king of Spain owing to her informal network of dashing and seafaring adventurers. By the liberal use of letters of marque, she created hundreds of privateers who stole for the state and were handsomely rewarded for basically carrying on like pirates. Liz was the last monarch of the House of Tudor and the grandmother of the British empire. She infamously never married, but her love of Francis Drake, Walter Raleigh, and robbing Spanish gold was legendary.

1579

In his prime, Sir Francis Drake loots the equivalent of $7 million from the Spanish ship *Nuestra Señora de la Concepción*, nicknamed *Cagafuego* ("fireshitter") for its furious firepower.

1647

The Putney Debates are held after the English Civil War. With King Charles I under house arrest in Hampton Court, the idea of universal suffrage is discussed and modern citizenship born as the soldiers and officers of Oliver Cromwell's New Model Army ponder how a country might be governed without a monarch. This milestone in democracy was lost to history for decades, but at the time these ideas were inspiring and empowering for those who witnessed them. Some of Cromwell's men were rewarded with positions in the Caribbean and may have sowed the seeds of suffrage that the pirates pillaged for their ships.

1664

New Amsterdam is renamed New York after the English beat the Dutch out of town and decide to name the bustling city after the Duke of York.

1667

Henry Morgan is handed his first letter of marque, granting him royal permission to attack and loot ships, starting life as a privateer, which in time led him to piracy.

1671

Henry Morgan leads the largest ever pirate action, heading a force of 2,000 in the audacious and unprecedented sacking of Panama, allegedly having failed to receive the memo that Britain is now at peace with Spain. This decimation of a strategic Spanish stronghold by an English-led force set a precedent whose waves were felt all the way to the formation of the British empire.

1678

The Buccaneers of America: A True Account of the Most Remarkable Assaults Committed of Late Years upon the Coast of the West Indies by the Buccaneers of Jamaica and Tortuga by Alexandre Exquemelin is published. Exquemelin is then promptly sued by Henry Morgan on the grounds that it is not such a true account after all. But what was true to life were the articles or code that Exquemelin set down. Henry Morgan's articles were therefore the first recorded use of the Pirate Code, a raft of policies and principles that were applied consistently throughout the Golden Age of Piracy to hold crew members accountable.

1687

Isaac Newton supposedly watches an apple fall from a tree and discovers gravity.

1690

The first pirate republic in Madagascar begins to settle and will become the first republic on earth with a written constitution declaring all men equal regardless of color.

1691

Pirate/privateer Admiral William Dampier completes his first of three circumnavigations of the globe and begins writing his memoirs, which would later be used by Captain Cook, Horatio Nelson, and Charles Darwin. Dampier also stands out as a most unusual pirate for his significant contribution to the English language, with over eighty words cited to his provenance, his contributions ranging from *avocado* to *barbecue* to *chopstick*.

1701

Captain Kidd is tried and hanged for piracy after unsuccessfully attempting to deny his entire career as a pirate by saying the stories were made up by "perjured and wicked people."

1707

[ISH]

First known use of the Pirate Flag, aka the Skull and Crossbones, aka the Jolly Roger, aka the Black, aka Surrender or Die, aka the world's first global superbrand.

1710

Benjamin Hornigold grows a following for his vision of a pirate republic, taking the democratic organizing principles they used aboard their ships onto land at Nassau in the Bahamas.

1713

The end of the Spanish War of Succession, which marks the start of the third and busiest period of the Golden Age of Piracy.

1717

Woodes Rogers, the ultimate anti-pirate, is commissioned to crush piracy. Rogers is an ex-privateer

who knows the pirates' tricks. A dead brother to avenge
and some arch-villain facial scars secured him the starring
role in kicking the pirates out of Nassau.

1718

Blackbeard is killed by a specially commissioned naval
fleet led by Lt. Robert Maynard. Blackbeard's headless
body is said to have swum three times around the
boats. Upon the capture of his ship, correspondence
bearing a royal emblem is found, identifying an ongoing
commercial and personal relationship between
Blackbeard and King George I's colonial governors in
America.

1719

Robinson Crusoe by Daniel Defoe is published. The book
is inspired by the rescue of Alexander Selkirk by Woodes
Rogers. Originally the book credited the fictional
character of Robinson Crusoe as the author, fooling
many at the time into believing that the events were real.
In so doing, the bestselling book marked the beginning
of realistic fiction as a literary genre, created a genre of
its own (about desert island castaways), and went on to
become one of the most adapted books of all time.

1724

A General History of the Robberies and Murders of the Most Notorious Pyrates is published, written by Charles Johnson, whom everyone wrongly assumes is Daniel Defoe. It becomes an immediate bestseller and is already on its fourth edition by 1726.

1771

Robert Owen, the father of the cooperative movement, is born less than twenty miles from the hometown of the pirate legend Henry Morgan. Owen dedicated his life to instilling the well-trodden pirate practices of fair pay, equal say, shared ownership, and social insurance that went on to influence modern business.

1773

The Boston Tea Party takes place. Republicans disguised as Mohawk Indians steal aboard English ships belonging to the East India Company and toss 342 casks of highly taxed tea into the sea, thereby setting into effect a course of events that led to American independence from English rule.

1832

The Skull and Bones secret soiety is formed at Yale
University and has since seen some of the world's most
powerful people through its doors, including both
presidents Bush.

1883

Robert Louis Stevenson releases *Treasure Island*,
introducing the world to Captain Flint, Billy Bones, and
Long John Silver. This has become one of the most
dramatized books of all time, with embellishments such
as black spots, parrots on shoulders, X-marked treasure
maps, and plank-walking defining the modern perception
of pirates forever.

1887

Coca-Cola creates "the world's first global superbrand"
when it registers its now ubiquitous logo roughly 180
years after the pirates invented the Skull and Crossbones
branding.

1904

J. M. Barrie's play *Peter Pan, or The Boy Who Wouldn't Grow Up*, opens in London, building on *Treasure Island* to compound the world's understanding of what it means to be a pirate with the introduction of Captain Hook.

1960s

Radio Caroline defines the idea of pirate radio, breaking the BBC monopoly of the airwaves by broadcasting some half-decent music from a ship anchored just outside UK jurisdiction.

1981

The United Nations recognizes the principles of the Open Sea, based on the exact sentiment Golden Age pirates argued and fought for nearly three hundred years earlier.

1983

Steve Jobs hosts an offsite day with the team working on the first Mac computers and delivers the immortal line "I'd rather be a pirate than join the navy" to inspire the direction of what would become the world's most valuable company. When Jobs died forty years after founding Apple, a flag bearing a skull and crossbones was raised over its headquarters.

1984

The wreck of the *Whydah*, the only authenticated pirate ship to be discovered, is found off Cape Cod. It had been the vessel of "Black" Sam Bellamy when it was sunk in a storm in 1717 on his way to visit his witch lover (!) and has since provided a veritable treasure trove of knowledge about the pirate way of life.

2008

Facebook adds Pirate into its platform as a legitimate language any user can choose. The software update was launched to celebrate International Talk Like a Pirate

Day and will translate most common languages into hackneyed Pirate verse.

2009

The Invisible Hook, Peter Leeson's examination of the economics of piracy, wins *Foreword Reviews*'s Gold Medal Book of the Year Award in Business and Economics.

2012

The *Pirates of the Caribbean* franchise has three films in the top twenty highest-grossing films of all time. (Marvel Universe, *Star Wars* reboots, and some better James Bond films have since pushed all the *Pirates of the Caribbean* films out of the top twenty.)

2016

The World Economic Forum convenes a specialist counsel to look at the effects of Blockchain technology, and the various cryptocurrencies it inspired. A full eight years after its launch, the establishment navy began to take this particular pirate seriously. One suspects they are going to wish they'd been a bit faster in getting ahead of this one.

2017

After a seven-year legal battle, the European Court of Justice makes a landmark ruling that the Pirate Bay file-sharing site is directly infringing copyright. Many commentators think it could spell the end of the Bay, which proves many commentators still profoundly misunderstood online piracy.

2018

Fragments of pages recovered from the wreckage of Blackbeard's ship, *Queen Anne's Revenge*, are found to be part of a popular real-life adventure book entitled *A Voyage to the South Sea, and Round the World*, partly disproving a previously held notion that pirates were largely illiterate, and showing that at least some of them enjoyed a good read.

Part Two

MAKING A PIRATE

Part Two

MAKING A PIRATE

4. REBELS WITH A CAUSE

Or How to Draw Strength by Standing Up to the Status Quo

Being a Rebel Is as Big a Deal as It Sounds

But it can also start out as a reassuringly small step. Becoming a rebel is the first decisive move you need to take to be more pirate, and all you have to do to begin is pick a rule to break. As we'll see in the next chapter, you've got to be willing to replace this rule with something better, but for now, you just need to be ready to cause a little good trouble, to pick at a few unfair edges, to question pointless or nonsensical rules, and when you have the chance, when rebellion will mean positive change, to do exactly the opposite of what you're told.

We need to get comfortable being uncomfortable. We need to be ready to break conventions that constrain our truths and get used to being scared by what we want to say and then saying it anyway. Changing your mind-set to embrace uncomfortable conversations is essential if you're going to alter the course of anything. Whether it's the bullying you encounter and ignore, the prejudice you witness but can no longer stand, the stories behind the front-page news that you just can't believe anymore, or the thought of showing up for yet another day in that place you despise—whatever it is that you feel the need to improve or change, you've got to target it at its very foundations.

Whether it's raising your voice, making a complaint, asking the difficult question, or point-blank refusing to follow even a small but stupid rule, the size of the first step has got to suit *you*. It's too early on your pirate journey to get thrown overboard straightaway. Your rebellion can start simple and build over enough time to enact change. The right level of rebellion should scare you just enough to make you feel alive but not so much that you are frozen. And when the deed is done, the email sent, the graffiti sprayed, the fuse lit, or the words spoken aloud... even if nothing changes immediately, if it takes a while for the revolution to kick in, you'll know your act of rebellion was targeted enough, and just big enough because you'll feel a little taller for having stood up for what you know is right, in the way that's right, against that which you knew was wrong.

No matter how small the first step, the fact that you made it intentionally is a huge deal. Get ready to go forth, my pirate, and enjoy the swell of pride you deserve for questioning a status quo. The challenges we face in our own lives and the big problems facing the world as we move into the ever more turbulent twenty-first century aren't going to be solved by doing things the way we've always done them, because that's precisely what got us here in the first place. It's no longer enough to resist; it's time to rebel.

There is nothing more troubling to any power system than the rebel who simply refuses to play the game, especially if they've got a far better game going on that's attracting followers, and they aren't afraid to shout about it. Golden Age pirates were dubbed "enemies of humanity" not because they were more morally corrupt than anyone else at the time but because their commitment to self-determination and collective action smelled like rebellion, at a time when around the world, the scent of revolution hung in the air.

Acclaimed historian Marcus Rediker describes how it's in the interest of any empire-building state to demote pirates from hero to villain: "No matter who or what he actually was, the pirate was reduced to criminal, pure and simple, the very negation of imperial social order."[1]

The author, teacher, and poet Kester Brewin expands Rediker's observation in his marvelous and amusing book *Mutiny! Why We Love Pirates, and How They Can Save Us*: it was, in royal eyes, quite acceptable to plunder other ships and steal their booty, as long as that was being done for the furtherance of the empire, so long as riches were still being channeled back to the capital. Pirates were "the very negation of imperial social order" precisely because to turn pirate they had raised two fingers at those who commanded them. It wasn't their thievery that was so heinous, so unutterably villainous, but their self-determination and refusal to be governed.[2]

The primal power of pirates, wherever and whenever we find them, is in their embodiment of the threat of rebellion. To be a pirate, you must call time on nonsense and commit to call out whoever is in charge when they make up rules that suck.

At this stage it doesn't matter if you don't have a fully worked-up plan for sparking change. For now, commit to making good trouble on a regular basis and you can trust that big change will soon be knocking.

It doesn't matter if you want to change something small, like the way someone behaves that's been driving you mad, or if your rebellion is in aid of something far grander affecting a much broader community than you. Margaret Wheatley, an expert in subverting systems, says, "All social change begins with a conversation."[3] So whether you want to rebel in a big or a small way, the first step you need to take is to start a conversation about it, whatever *it* is, with *whoever* can help.

In this chapter we'll be looking at examples of modern-day pirates and their Golden Age predecessors who drew strength from calling out the hypocrisy, failure, or injustice they saw around them. We'll see how these acts of defiance can build momentum and cause ripples that spark cultural and societal change. And if that sounds daunting, remember that everything starts from a simple act of defiance, which at its most basic can be summed up as the impulse to disagree with and defy those pretending they know what they're doing. The Golden Age pirates called it "going on the account" when they ditched their old and abusive employer and went pirate. Just to be clear, I'm not advocating you all quit doing what you do tomorrow, but I am saying that there's huge power in declaring to yourself (and your crew or teammates) that you've hijacked the ship, changed course, and are now fully accountable for your own actions.

Holding Out for a Hero

If I'm going to present to you just one example of a Golden Age pirate who embraced the idea of rebellion to its core, and I am, then I'd be remiss not to serve you up Captain "Black" Sam Bellamy. The youngest of six, born into poverty and potential obscurity in Devon, Bellamy slogged through his teens in the terrible conditions of the Royal Navy before turning pirate in 1715. His career lasted barely two years, cut short when he and most of his crew were drowned just off Cape Cod, but despite his brief stint on the high seas, Bellamy managed to become the richest pirate in recorded history, being dubbed the Prince of Pirates for his merciful treatment of captives and the Robin Hood of the Sea for the generosity with which he treated his crew, who proudly referred to themselves as Robin Hood's men. And all this by the age of twenty-eight.

Articulate, dashing, charismatic, and intelligent, Black Sam was clearly a formidable captain and a successful strategist, but he was also a much-loved leader whose impassioned defense of the pirate life helped generate respect for the pirate cause. He is consequently the go-to pirate for a rousing speech to raise us up against the institutions that hold us back. Printed in Captain Charles Johnson's *A General History of the Robberies and Murders of the Most Notorious Pyrates* (1724) was a memorable speech delivered by Black Sam to the captain of a merchant ship he had just captured who had declined the pirate's invitation to go on the account because his conscience would not allow him to break the laws of God or man. Black Sam didn't hesitate to point out his fellow captain's hypocrisy and delusion in a blistering piece of antiestablishment rhetoric that appalled and terrified the authorities of the day:

Damn ye, you are a sneaking puppy, and so are all those who will submit to be governed by laws which rich men have made for their own security, for the cowardly whelps have not the courage otherwise to defend what they get by their knavery, but damn ye altogether: damn them for a pack of crafty rascals, and you, who serve them, for a parcel of hen-hearted numbskulls. . . . They vilify us, the Scoundrels do, when there is only this Difference: They rob the Poor under the Cover of Law, forsooth, and we plunder the Rich under the Protection of our own Courage; had you not better make one of us, than sneak off after the asses of those villains for employment? . . . I am a free Prince, and I have as much Authority to make War on the whole World, as he who has a hundred Sail of Ships at Sea, and an Army of 100,000 Men in the Field . . . but there is no arguing with such snivelling Puppies, who allow Superiors to kick them about Deck at Pleasure; and pin their Faith upon a Pimp of a Parson; a Squab, who neither practises nor believes what he puts upon the chuckle-headed Fools he preaches to.[4]

Black Sam goes hard, and does not go home. In one fell swoop he challenges the government, the law, the emerging big businesses of the time, and even the spirituality being used by the church as a form of social control. Listing their abuses of power and the damage done to the common man, he puts himself on a level playing field with these enormous enemies, and then by taking them down, elevates himself above them. It's an incredibly effective technique both for undermining your enemies and for strengthening your support base.

It was these powerful sentiments of rebellion, well-articulated, exciting, and inspiring challenges circulating in the newspapers, taprooms, and gossip columns throughout Europe and the New World, that eventually became too much for the establishment to bear. That such a clear clarion call for rebellion came from the meeting point of the world's superpowers in the heart of the Caribbean made it even more of an anti-colonial kick in the teeth. Eventually, when the promise of escalating rebellion became impossible to ignore, when the pirates had all but won the battle for the hearts and minds of the people, the physical pirate threat was vanquished in the obliteration of the Republic of Pirates on Nassau. But it turned out to be much, much too late to stuff the genie back in the bottle. The principles of the pirate change-effect had become clear and were being carefully co-opted and adopted by the general public, policymakers, and powers that be, and are still in play today.

The message for all of us as individuals is clear: the echo of a deftly made act of defiance can be heard around the world. Shaping your idea into a rebellious shout, or even just a firm no, can make you feel brave enough to do it again and again. And when we say no, not just as individuals but as collectives, then even the world's largest, most immovable institutions listen.

From Golden Age Pirates to Pirate Radio to the Pirate Bay

Over the last sixty years, numerous began-in-a-bedroom rebellions have ended up changing entire industries. New technologies and discoveries have spurred endless disputes between the old order and nimble rebels who grew tired of being ignored and eventually opted to do things their own way.

One example of an industry that was forever changed by a small group of rebels who actually call themselves pirates is the entertainment industry. Starting in the UK, the era of mass media began just after World War I, when a consortium of businesses investing in early radio consumables got together to found the country's first broadcasting company. Knowing an idea worth stealing when they saw one, the government assumed ownership to create what is now the BBC. For an entire generation a state-backed monopoly controlled the airwaves with a firm hand and a narrow choice of channels articulating its values to educate, inform, and entertain. But, if your idea of being entertained, informed, and educated involved new music, alternative culture, independent artists, modern drama, or anything without a stiff upper lip, you weren't being catered to. Imagine having a binary choice of radio stations with a heavy bias on classical music or gardening programs as your ONLY domestic source of aural fun at the height of the swinging sixties.

When market conditions don't provide options that meet the needs of the people, pirates appear at the edges to explore alternatives and force the mainstream to adopt their ideas. And so it was that in 1964, pirate radio sailed into view. Literally. Radio Caroline launched the era of pirate radio from a boat off the south coast, sidestepping the law of the land by broadcasting from international waters. The DJs were cool, the formats were casual, the vibe was rebelliously commercial. It was innovation, it was revolution on a ship outside the law but in range of your radio.

Within two years there were a dozen pirate broadcasters being listened to by a third of the population, and as advertisers followed, the threat of all-out radio rebellion eventually forced the BBC to offer more choice by adding their own imitative channels.

Although this rebellion led to change, at the same time the government came down hard on the rebels, pushing pirate radio underground, off the high seas, and into high-rise tower blocks. This sparked decades of running battles between regulators and pirate broadcasters.

As with the Golden Age pirates, the moral argument against radio pirates was flawed, and the need for the establishment to adapt was proven, but still the state could not allow itself to be undermined by their existence. A combination of harsh repression, an amnesty, and limited legal licenses, but ultimately, the inclusion of pirate practices into the mainstream finally brought about an end to what some would consider another Golden Age. Pirate radio's creativity, sense of community, and contribution to culture continues, with pirate stations thriving online, although not perhaps with the same threat of rebellion they once posed.

Nothing epitomizes the individuals behind pirate radio's intention to cause good trouble while having fun than this quote from *Radio Is My Bomb: A DIY Manual for Pirates*, published by the sublimely named Hooligan Press in 1987:

This is intended as a Do-It-Yourself Pirate's Handbook, aimed at promoting neighbourhood, political and open-

access radio pirates . . . But obviously you can use it as you
wish. You can build the transmitters and use them to jam
out Aunty Beeb, you can play your favourite music, or you
can set up local open-access stations as we suggest . . . Or
you can set up a fascist station and we'll come and kick
your heads in![5]

It's all here in this quote: the defining note of disobedience that
scares the powers that be, the proud sense of self-governance
that is at the core of being more pirate, and the rebel's call that
captures and builds momentum and attracts followers. In *The
Pirate's Dilemma: How Youth Culture Is Reinventing Capitalism*,
Matt Mason establishes the clear link between the Golden Age
pirates and those early pirates of radio: "Pirate radio, in other
words, *is* pirate, through and through. Its DNA runs back
through the seafaring rebels who fought for just treatment and
an equal voice. Piracy has gone on throughout history, and we
should encourage it. It's how inefficient systems are replaced.
Wherever you tune in, somewhere you will find a pirate pushing back against authority, decentralizing monopolies, and promoting the rule of the people: the very nature of democracy
itself."[6]

Unsurprisingly, the pirate radio movement kept spread-
ing and picking up energy, inspiring future generations who
wanted to harness new technology to access culture in more
open ways. It inspired the beginnings of digital piracy.

Twenty-First-Century New World

The digital world of the twenty-first century is even more vast than the New World of Latin America, the Caribbean, and the dis-United States were during the Golden Age. Admittedly there's a bit less looting of indigenous populations' resources, but both worlds represent new frontiers, new rules, and new potential for forging unimaginable wealth.

With the advent of a new digital world, piracy once again innovated from the edges and taught the mainstream a lesson before being equally outlawed and appropriated as usual. Early file-sharing sites like Napster and LimeWire created a market for online music and paved the way for iTunes and the multibillion-dollar online music industry that followed it. "You've got your head up your asses," said Steve Jobs when talking to the heads of the music industry who were trying to sue and shut down every illegal file-sharing music piracy website that had destroyed physical CD sales, while offering audiences no alternative. To prove his point, Jobs launched the iTunes store in April 2003 with the backing, if not the understanding, of the record industry and a target to make a million sales in six months. iTunes sold 6 million units in one week. Mass-scale music piracy was not dead and buried, but it was certainly finally rivaled because the industry responded to the pirates' threat that was being fed by an audience of millions who wanted choice.

Sites like the Pirate Bay demonstrated the vast opportunity for film sharing and streaming that helped chart a course for Netflix, iPlayer, and Hulu to follow. Silk Road, the go-to portal for the sale of illegal and contraband goods and services, set new standards in peer-reviewed e-commerce that even the likes of online retailing giants eBay, Amazon, and Alibaba had something to learn from. Blockchain technology and the various cryptocurrencies it sits behind like Bitcoin also carry the scent of rebellion, this time challenging the financial industry by threatening the need for one, as the role of the broker in any given transaction is effectively made redundant. The huge significance of online currencies is only just emerging, but the pattern of pirate history suggests they will be game-changing for an industry that will be forced to adapt and adopt what was once radical and revolutionary into the mainstream.

This perspective was neatly crystallized by author and activist Lawrence Lessig in his book *Free Culture: The Nature and Future of Creativity*:

Every generation welcomes the pirates from the last. If "piracy" means using the creative property of others without their permission—if "if value, then right" is true— then the history of the content industry is a history of piracy. Every important sector of "big media" today—film, records, radio, and cable TV—was born of a kind of piracy so defined. The consistent story is how last generation's pirates join this generation's country club—until now.[7]

Digital transformation is a wave that has carried and will continue to carry fleets of pirates. But my reason for drawing on the development of new twenty-first-century technologies is less about charting the achievements of modern pirates and more about showcasing the fundamental power of carefully chosen acts of rebellion. The first step toward making positive change is to question, challenge, and go beyond. A rebellious mind-set is key to innovation and the first of five tactics you need to command on your journey to being more pirate. Along the way, you will also need some twenty-first-century pirate contemporaries to take inspiration from. Luckily, there are already some legends we can look to.

A Modern Pirate Called Malala

When the whole world is silent, even one voice becomes powerful.

—Malala Yousafzai

I appreciate that Malala Yousafzai's might not be the first name you'd expect to see here, but I'm outing her as a twenty-first-century pirate because there are few examples that exemplify the first stage of the pirate change as well as she does.

Undermining an entire fundamentalist movement deemed terrorists by most Western governments all by yourself isn't every schoolgirl's idea of a good time. But Malala's stand against the Taliban in Pakistan illustrates the infinite power of the rebel. She was one individual against an army, a schoolgirl against armed men. Her power came from defying the army, challenging their ideals, and refusing to stay silent.

In 2009, as an eleven-year-old girl, Malala started a blog where she wrote about girls' rights to education. Her blog gained traction, and as a consequence *The New York Times* made a documentary about her life during the Taliban occupation of Swat. As Malala was gaining more exposure as an activist and public opposer of those in power, she was shot in the head by the Taliban in 2012. Thankfully, she survived.

Malala became a figurehead for human rights activism and went on to found a nonprofit organization that helps girls access education, write a book, and receive the Nobel Peace Prize in 2014. Whether it's the front cover of her bestseller, her UN speech, or the posters for the film of her life, her message is clear: one girl against an entire regime, conveying the paradoxical strength of a child. Or in her words: "If one man can destroy everything, why can't one girl change it?"

Malala's story is exceptional and her achievements are huge. But her initial action was a very small act of rebellion. The act of writing a blog has become humdrum and might not feel like rebellion enough for you, but the content of Malala's blogs was radical within the context of her environment. The action is something that any of us can do so long as we have an internet connection. One girl, one blog, one idea: accessible and rebellious.

Rebellion might seem messy and scary, and that's because it is. Standing up to something or someone can be daunting, uncomfortable, or awkward, and that's because it is. But it is also the essential first step toward making change. Asking questions and challenging the status quo can get you into trouble, but we're talking about good trouble here—the sort of trouble you can be proud of, the sort of trouble you'll want to tell your children you took a stand for. The sort of trouble that can save you from being that person who was "just following orders." If you're looking for change, big or small, if you'd like things to look different tomorrow or next year, then you need to take a deep breath and break some rules, because it's only among a little chaos that we find the best beginnings of new creation and opportunity.

Give me freedom or give me the rope. For I shall not take the shackles that subjugate the poor to uphold the rich.

—John Goldenwolf

Causing good trouble requires confidence in your own ability to stand up to power and then holding your nerve to actually see it through.

Even when your rebellion is a really small step, we're so hardwired to play by the rules, it can seem impossibly hard to take your stand.

That is until we remind ourselves we've all done it, how good it felt, and that of course we can all do it again and again.

In this chapter we've seen how small acts and big change come from the same place, but in order to begin you have to know where the source of your power lies as an individual.

What follows is a challenge that really resonates in our workshops; its usefulness is not immediately obvious to everyone, but it reconnects most people with their power to take a stand.

So the challenge this time is to look into your memory and ask:

When did you first stand up to power?

Give yourself a chance to let this one sink in, as I appreciate it's not something you might have thought about before in this way or might immediately remember, but give it time and you will.

Try to find the moment or moments when you first understood your own influence or when you clearly saw your own potential to create and shape the world around you.

When I've run this exercise in the Be More Pirate workshops, the answers are usually focused on a time when a person has stood up to something or someone they felt was being unjust, when they've pushed back, when they've fought their corner, held their nerve, or just said no, and in return the world gave way, backed down, yielded, or said sorry.

Often there's an instance in life when someone has found their voice and others listened, or a moment when a relationship has shifted, or when someone has just point-blank refused to do as they were told and got away with it.

Mine was in primary school. I must have been eight, and after it happened, the class and the teacher fell silent for what felt like minutes, before I was sent to the head teacher for a punishment that never materialized. A lifetime later, I can point to this exact moment when I lost all fear of authority. I realized there isn't anyone you can't squirt in the eye with a water pistol if you really want to.

It doesn't matter how big or small the action was, what counts is that in that moment you realized your own power amid the context of the world. The point is that we all have the power we need and we've all felt it; we just allow it to be forgotten, we choose not to live with it, and as you're going to be using it soon, it may need a kick start. So first try to remember what it felt like, and then remind yourself to use it.

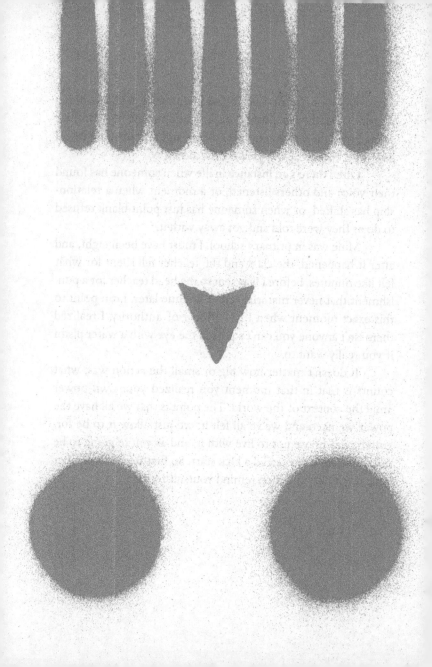

5. REWRITE YOUR RULES

Or How to Bend, Break, and Ultimately Rewrite the Rules

Mutiny and the Bounty

The pirates of the Golden Age changed the game, rewrote the rules, and altered the course of history. Unlike so much of the innovation at the birth of the Industrial Revolution, where earnest men with large furrowed brows sweated diligently over steam engines, pirates didn't change the world by purposeful invention, they did it through wilful obstruction that challenged all the rules of the time. And in setting out to break something, they ended up making something. They didn't just want to tear down the old order; they wanted to create something better for themselves.

This is what distinguishes them from other forms of rebels, punks, and rogues, and makes them more akin to unconscious artists, architects, and creators than chaos merchants. And it is their gift to you: being more pirate permits you to find creativity through destruction. In this chapter we'll move beyond their fearlessness in questioning bad rules that weren't working to look at how their actions led to the creation of new rules. We'll see that there's power in stepping outside anachronistic structures and challenging broken systems that benefit only the few with new ideas that can benefit and inspire the many.

A utopian vision of the future wasn't the pirates' top priority. They were focused on the more classic pirate pastimes of rum, treasure, and not getting hanged, but by rejecting the status quo they ignited a spark and showed an alternative that caused like minds to gather and form around new ideas that filled the smoking hole they'd left in the wake of their rebellion. That's what this chapter is about: the formation of new ideas that capture others' imagination; the early creation of better rules that people choose to gather around and that represent the beginning of a new belonging; and a challenge to the idea that accepting what we've got is good enough.

The pirates weren't the first people to raze things to the ground to allow glorious new creations to flourish. Throughout history, the most radically successful ideas derived at least some of their appeal from a rejection of the old ways. As Picasso famously said, "Every act of creation is first an act of destruction."

The point is (and to be frank, this applies whether you're an artist, a poet, a pirate, a pawn, a pauper, or a king), sometimes confronting, questioning, obstructing, destroying, smashing, bending, and breaking even just one thing is a legitimate and useful way of creating change. The greatest change-makers know this, but they also know that you can't get stuff done on a big scale by breaking rules alone. You have to provide an alternative. You have to change the game and rewrite the rules.

The pirates had a term for this. Obviously it's not as beautifully expressed as Picasso's words, but it will help us be clear in our intent, and it's the term we're going to use, because it's the act you're going to take . . . the word is *mutiny*.

Mutiny is how pirates took rebellion and turned it into a new set of rules that others could follow. On Wikipedia, mutiny is described as "a conspiracy among a group of people to openly oppose, change, or overthrow an authority to which they are subject,"[1] which is exactly what we're looking for, but is also not as scary or likely to get you arrested as it sounds.

Mutiny is the route to writing new rules, the bridge between the act of destruction and the act of creation, and the gravitational force that will help pull other pirates to your cause.

Once we've looked at how pirates, past and present, have rewritten the rule book in a way that gathered "the brethren," you'll be one step closer to designing your own mutiny and growing your own crew.

And remember, when we talk about mutiny, we're not talking about sailing 10,000 miles, braving sea monsters and storms to risk hanging for stealing Spanish gold. We're just talking about standing up for what you believe in, whether that's doing something different at work, making a shift in a serious relationship, being the agent for change in your local community, or even actually doing something about that idea you've been thinking about but are not acting upon. They are all mutinies worth starting, and starting now. A mutiny of trying something out, making something happen, doing something different, or beginning something.

There was a time (and I know, because I was there) before the side hustle, when doing your own thing and starting something new meant building the "business plan" for it, convincing a bank manager to support it, getting incorporated, and other long-winded hurdles to clear. But luckily for you, those days are long gone. Now, in the pretotyping age, all it takes is self-belief and an internet connection to spark a movement, begin a project, make a difference, or even start a company.

Pretotyping? Yup, it's the stage before prototyping, and it's a great way of saying "making it up" with a sort of professional ring to it. Alberto Savoia, the man who came up with Google's law of failure, designed the Pretotyping Manifesto (look it up) as a guide for embracing the tools around us to invent the stuff of the future without needing to invest much money or time.[2] Whether you're in an organization trying to introduce new products or attitudes to old mind-sets, or flying solo trying to create a new service or goods, there has never been so much opportunity afforded you to try stuff out in real life; it's never been easier to start a project or test a product idea, whether it's a podcast or a pop-up, a performance or a political act; if you really wanted to, you could call a mutiny on the rules of today and have new rules under way by this time tomorrow.

The Golden Age pirates seized the unique opportunities on offer to them and instigated mutinies to pave the way for new rules that would improve their life. Modern pirates do the same, replacing old rules with new rules and bad ideas with good ones. In the same way the last chapter made rebellion digestible if taken with a hearty meal, this chapter will illustrate how to rewrite rules by looking to both eighteenth- and twenty-first-century pirates for inspiration.

Break the Biggest Rule You Know: The Remarkable Tale of Anne Bonny and Mary Read

It was never going to be hard to find examples of rule-breaking or rule-remaking pirates, but take your marks and get set for the story of Anne Bonny and Mary Read, pirate pioneers and proto-feminists whose game-changing influence is more profound than you can possibly imagine. These two women broke one of the most universal and stringently enforced rules of their society—the one that said women were not fully autonomous human beings with rights, responsibilities, and abilities equal to men. By setting off to sea, they contributed to one of the most far-reaching (if slow-moving and unfinished) revolutions our world has ever seen: the battle for equal rights. Bonny's and Read's stories prove just what can be achieved when you ask why not, take risks, find allies in your cause, and demonstrate to others that everything they assumed was wrong. Their rule-shattering and paradigm-shifting life stories would make for an excellent movie.

Bonny was born Anne McCormac in 1702, a by-product of her father's affair with the family maid. Disgraced, Dad, maid, and baby Anne moved from Ireland to London and then on to Carolina, where Anne grew up angry but, by all accounts, beautiful. As a teenager she married small-time pirate James Bonny in secret, thinking it better to seek forgiveness rather than permission. Her plan backfired and her father kicked her and her new husband out onto the streets. When James realized that without her father's financial patronage, Anne was worth "not a groat" and, worse still, was now his expense, he was ready to hit the road.³

Jack, the dashing pirate captain Calico Jack Rackham, who'd been swashbuckling up and down the eastern seaboard with a larger-than-life pirate swagger, chose this moment to arrive on the scene. Jack charmed the bloomers off Bonny, and offered her the opportunity to deliver the ultimate "middle finger" to polite society by running away with him, a handsome "enemy of humanity" and one of the foremost Golden Age pirates.

First, Bonny attempted to exploit a legal loophole to free her from her former vows so that she could marry Rackham and make a mockery of marriage laws that viewed her as her absent husband's property. She threatened violence on the noncompliant official who rejected her attempts and then blew a hole the size of a pirate ship in accepted female conventions and ran away to sea with her lover to live as a pirate. As Johnson put it in his *A General History of the Robberies and Murders of the Most Notorious Pyrates*, she and Calico Jack "finding they could not by fair means enjoy each other's company with Freedom, resolved to run away together and enjoy it inspite [sic] of all the world."[4]

Back in England, Mary Read's not dissimilar story began to gather pace. Mary had also been born an illegitimate child, but before she was even born, her father had abandoned her mother and their newborn son, Mark, who died shortly afterward. To complicate matters, Mary's mother discovered she was pregnant with Mary shortly after her husband had disappeared. . . . In need of a way to disguise her condition from the world and from her mother-in-law, who was obliged to support her financially, Mary pretended her baby daughter was a boy and passed her off as her dead brother.

An early life of pretending to be a man became a habit, and the teenage Mary joined the army, which women were of course forbidden to do. As Mark, she became a fierce fighter and a distinguished soldier, and fell deeply in love with one of her comrades-in-arms. What eighteenth-century awkwardness ensued no one will ever know, but somehow, some night, in some European conflict, in some army tent somewhere, Mary must have revealed she was indeed a lady, because we know that love flourished between the soldiers. Due to their hard-fought reputation for good service and their renowned bravery—and of course the dazzlingly good story it made to tell the folks back home—the couple were celebrated and Mary was spared the punishment she technically deserved for deceiving the army command.

As it happened, the army command abso-bloody-lutely loved it. Their superior officers didn't just approve their request to be married, they paid for the party and invited themselves along. Following which, Mary and her man were discharged with full honors and given help to buy a local pub that became a firm favorite with the soldiers stationed nearby.

But the eighteenth century was harsh as hell, and Mary's husband promptly died of a hideous eighteenth-century blood-curdling disease. The pub trade took a downturn and then— sad, mad, penniless, and alone—Mary went back to wearing men's clothes and once again illegally signed on. This time around, however, Mary joined the Royal Navy and before long was captured at sea by pirates. Reluctantly, or so the story goes, Mary gave in to the pirate life and was unsurprisingly rather good at it. As she moved up the ranks and from ship to ship, Mary aka Mark one day found she'd joined the crew of a certain Anne Bonny and Jack Rackham. (See what I meant when I said it would make a good movie.)

Soon enough, another member of the crew caught Mary's eye, and she once again had to reveal herself to her new fancy to win his affections, and once again fell deeply in love. Time passed and her new man got himself into a spot of bother gambling. As per the Pirate Code of that particular crew, he had to settle the dispute in a duel on the beach. Mary, an accomplished swordswoman, judged her sweetheart the likely loser of the ensuing contest, and so stepped in. Before the beefing buccaneers could cut loose with their cutlasses, Mary gave it a De Niro dose of "You looking at me?" and skewered her lover's rival with her sword, then dumped his corpse overboard.

So far so very badass, but Anne and Mary aren't finished. Now a formidable duo, with the backing of Captain Jack, they sailed the seas side by side as Pirate Queens and became legends in their own lifetime.

Turning pirate was an active choice for Bonny and Read, a far more appealing alternative to the powerless and financially vulnerable position they would have been in had they stayed put on land and played by the book. They, like so many other pirates, preferred to make their own way in the world, following their own rules in how they contributed to the collective interest of their crew. The remarkable thing is that the pirate ship allowed them the freedom to do exactly that. At a time when women were held to be inferior to men in every way, intellectually, morally, and spiritually, Bonny and Read participated on the same level as their male counterparts in pirate life. Thomas Dillon, the master of a merchant vessel captured by the crew, observed that they "were both very profligate, cursing and swearing much, and very ready and willing to do anything on board."[5]

Both women blasted every conventional argument about women's qualities and capabilities out of the water, simply by being there and being themselves. Esteemed historian Marcus Rediker states that

> although [Bonny and Read were] not formally elected by their fellow pirates to posts of command, they nonetheless led by example—in fighting duels, in keeping the deck in time of engagement and in being part of the group designated to board prizes, a right always reserved for the most daring and respected members of the crew. [They] proved a woman could find liberty beneath the Jolly Roger.[6]

In other words, they rebelled and they rewrote the rules of what women could and couldn't do.

Bonny and Read's time together was short, and in less than a year Rackham's entire crew was targeted and taken down by the Royal Navy, which had an official warrant for the capture and execution of "Notorious Pirates" including Bonny and Read, the first and only female pirates named on any warrant during the Golden Age. When the navy caught up with Rackham's crew, it arrived in such a considerable force that the men of the pirate crew took cover below while Bonny and Read remained on deck, hurling abuse and shooting their pistols at both the advancing navy and their cowardly comrades.

When the day was done, the navy defeated the Pirate Queens and the entire crew was taken to execution dock. After the trials, Jack was due to be hanged first, before which he was granted one last audience with his lover, whereupon Anne delivered to him the immortal line, "Sure, I'm sorry to see you here, but if you had fought like a man you need not have hanged like a dog." Ouch.

At this point the lives of Mary Read and Anne Bonny diverged. They both escaped the hangman's noose on the grounds that they were pregnant, but Mary died not long after in prison, possibly from complications in childbirth, and Anne and her child disappeared off the face of the earth, either ransomed by her father or perhaps sprung from prison by former pirate colleagues.

Though it would be overstepping the mark to claim that these remarkable, rebellious rule-breaking women were consciously striking a blow for any proto–women's movement, their story became part of a new conversation around women's capabilities and entitlements that was emerging at the time in both high and low culture. Their legend made its way into shanties and ballads, giving millions of mostly illiterate working-class women an intoxicating example of poor and marginalized women just like them who had lived life on their own terms. The story was jumped on by the emerging media, who hailed the pair as "warrior women"[7] on the front pages of the penny dreadfuls, the gossip magazines of the day. Mind you, though this coverage was sometimes admiring, it also came with a hefty dose of condemnation, as you would expect from figures who challenged some of society's most fundamental rules. Bonny and Read were heroines to some but were also vilified as shameless traitors to their sex.

As Rediker suggests, the famous pair found freedom under the Jolly Roger. He argues convincingly that none other than Anne Bonny is the inspiration for one of the most famous paintings of all time, *Le 28 Juillet. La Liberté guidant le peuple*, known in English as *Liberty Leading the People*, by Eugène Delacroix, painted in 1830.

One of the most influential pieces of art in the world, it hangs in the Louvre in Paris, as it always has, but chances are you've seen a poster version of it, as the promoters of the West End/Broadway show *Les Misérables* have adapted it for their own revolutionary purposes.

Rediker compares the defining portrait of Bonny that appeared in Captain Johnson's *General History of the Pyrates* with the enduring image of Lady Liberty; "a central female figure, armed, bare-breasted and dressed in a Roman tunic, looks back as she propels herself forward—upward, over, and above a mass of dead bodies."[8] They are a mirror image of each other, except where Bonny holds her sword above her head, Lady Liberty raises up a flag. Bonny is joined by a young man, Lady Liberty is accompanied by a boy. Rediker provides an arsenal of evidence to prove this is no coincidence, first that Delacroix was known to be fascinated by pirates and "endlessly inspired" by Lord Byron's famous long poem *The Corsair*, which he studied as he painted *La Liberté*. Rediker also points out that by this point, the *General History of the Pyrates* that had the portrait of Bonny on the cover was an international bestseller on its twentieth edition with at least six editions printed in French. As Rediker puts it, "it would be a fitting tribute to Bonny and Mary Read if the example of these two women who seized liberty beneath the Jolly Roger in turn helped to inspire one of the most famous depictions of liberty the modern world has ever known."[9]

Even if you weren't familiar with Delacroix's painting, the strong woman in robes looking out, striding forward, one arm raised, a symbol of hope and liberty sounds familiar? That's because it's the same composition as the Statue of Liberty in New York. Sure, the Statue of Liberty looks a bit more respectable and less revolutionary, with a few more clothes and a torch rather than a sword, but she was partly inspired by Delacroix's lady nonetheless. So it seems the Statue of Liberty is a distant relation of Anne Bonny the Pirate Queen . . .

If you can't quite picture the Delacroix painting, or you think I'm making all of this up, I've lined up the respective images for you; just go to www.bemorepirate.com/liberty and see for yourself.

In terms of rewriting the rule book, Bonny sets the bar pretty high. She influenced cultural depictions of freedom and reimagined the way women could and should act by refusing to accept the rules as they were. Bonny and Read's greatest power was in being themselves and leading by example, rejecting the prejudiced protocols of the day and charting their own course instead, a fundamental principle of a *Be More Pirate* mind-set.

The Tall Tales of Captain Elon Musk

When something is important enough, you do it even if the odds are not in your favor.

—Elon Musk, founder of PayPal, SpaceX, Tesla, and SolarCity, and possible supervillain

Elon Musk is a thoroughly modern pirate of seemingly limitless ambition. The man has something to prove. When it comes to rewriting rules, Musk is THE man to look to. Not content with first rewriting the rules of how we handle money with PayPal, how we perceive and use energy with Tesla and SolarCity, how we travel long distance with Hyperloop, he's now set on rewriting the rules of life as we know it via SpaceX and his mission to colonize Mars.

Just as we spoke about Malala in the previous chapter about rebellion, I want to remind you that it's important not to get daunted or distracted by Musk's massive scale of achievement. What's useful is to look at how Musk did what he did and plunder those methods of his that will serve us mere mortals. But let's start by assessing what's happened so far. Musk started his first software enterprise with his brother on a few thousand dollars, and sold it for several million a few years later. He quickly bought into a business that owned a small and neglected idea called PayPal. It didn't stay small and neglected for long. Musk took PayPal to the ubiquitous global brand and utility it is today, completely rewriting the rules of the global finance sector in the process. Then he walked away with $180 million. As he famously says, "My proceeds from the PayPal acquisition were $180 million. I put $100 million in SpaceX, $70 million in Tesla, and $10 million in SolarCity. I had to borrow money for rent."

With Tesla, Musk aims to popularize electric, environmentally friendly cars that can outperform a combustion-engined car on every level possible. With SolarCity he's set out to demonstrate we can power our lives without relying on fossil fuels, by fitting desirable solar panels on our homes that look the same as roof tiles. And with SpaceX he's proving a private company can advance quicker in space exploration than NASA, not to mention the small matter of trying to give humanity a chance of life on Mars. With Hyperloop, he released a fifty-seven-page open-source document detailing his plans for a transport system that would carry travelers from San Francisco to L.A. in a matter of minutes. Despite all the well-founded criticism that has come his way, his ambitious plans have won support around the world, with investors like Richard Branson helping to take the ideas further. Musk proves how open-sourcing your ideas starts to create followers for your new rules.

Like his pirate predecessors, Captain Musk is clearly up for adventure and deeply engaged with exploration. But for me, the root of Musk's pirate-like persona stems from his ambition to cause good trouble, to question first principles and rewrite the outcomes as a consequence. Musk finds solutions to big problems because he adopts the mental model of first principles in which you leave analogy-based argument behind and challenge all assumptions made. Musk calls it his "Scientific Method." For example, when Musk and his team were working out how much the first SpaceX rocket would cost them, instead of looking at comparable products and setting a benchmark accordingly, they figured out what the necessary parts of a rocket were and then found out how much the raw materials cost. They found that they could make a rocket at 2 percent of the normal cost. And all this because he questioned and challenged assumptions. Musk's success is wrapped up in how he's taken these findings and written new rules around them and published them as goals, or if you like, Pirate Codes to live and work by.

In 2006 Musk published the Master Plan for Tesla. This was quite unlike any conventional business plan. In the modern-day equivalent of a Golden Age pirate nailing articles to the ship's mast, he posted it online. It's pretty simple, but it encapsulates a way of doing business that builds in good trouble as a design principle and screams pirate in its delight in mischief-making. It reads:

1. Build sports car.
2. Use that money to build an affordable car.
3. Use *that* money to build an even more affordable car.
4. While doing above, also provide zero emission electric power generation options.
5. Don't tell anyone.

When you know what you're rebelling against, and you've got your idea and others who want to follow, if you want your new rules to stick, let others own them as theirs. Give them away freely for others to adopt, adapt, and believe in as if they were their own. By doing this, you make them complicit in your thinking, as it becomes their thinking. Rather than forcing his rules on others, Musk inspires people with his openness, and as a consequence his ideas permeate the mainstream faster.

Like Captain Benjamin Hornigold in the early 1700s, who had the vision for the Republic of Pirates as a new way of life, Musk is planning nothing less than a human colony on

Mars. Hornigold put out the call among the pirate brethren and shared his vision with the next generation of pirate leaders. And they came. Musk essentially does the same, laying down new rules for a new vision of the future:

> Fuck Earth! Who cares about Earth?
>
> There needs to be an intersection of the set of people who wish to go [to Mars], and the set of people who can afford to go . . . and that intersection of sets has to be enough to establish a self-sustaining civilization. My rough guess is that for a half-million dollars, there are enough people that could afford to go and would want to go.
>
> But it's not going to be a vacation jaunt. It's going to be saving up all your money and selling all your stuff, like when people moved to the early American colonies . . . even at a million people you're assuming an incredible amount of productivity per person, because you would need to re-create the entire industrial base on Mars.
>
> If we can establish a Mars colony, we can almost certainly colonize the whole Solar System, because we'll have created a strong economic forcing function for the improvement of space travel.[10]

Three hundred years after old Ben Hornigold said, "Fuck Society, let's take these great democratic principles we've made, reject this broken system and start a new way of life," and Musk is flying the same flag. He's laying down new rules for anyone to follow if they choose, and can afford half a million dollars!

The Fine Art of the Remix

If Musk has rewritten the rules of the energy industry by inventing a better battery, then hip-hop has rewritten the rules of the music industry by inventing a better beat. Hip-hop is and always has been about the remix, its own term for mutiny. Back in the early 1970s when DJ Kool Herc pulled off a previously unimaginable act, playing two copies of the same record simultaneously, looping and extending the drum section of the tune, the breakbeat was reinvented. With a longer backbeat from Herc, it was down to Afrika Bambaataa to add the lyrics. With these two pirates at the helm, hip-hop became the new voice of rebellion, bum-rushing the political jazz poetry that inspired it out of the way and bringing to life rap instead. When rap and breakbeat were joined by breakdance and graffiti, the so-called Four Elements of hip-hop were established and a new culture was born.

Hip-hop was a new rebel flag presenting a new way of operating that attracted others to join its movement. Hip-hop's success has been in part due to its dedication to reinvention; it somehow manages to convey the promise of transformation and reincarnation while also being unashamedly mainstream. Groups like Niggaz With Attitude, or N.W.A., went double platinum because of their global sales to middle-class young white boys desperate to drink in the rebel sounds of their wicked beats. Hard-hitting lyrics laced with profanity and misogyny, depicting the dark reality for young black men in America, were learned verbatim by English schoolboys as Compton became the new soundtrack to small towns from Key West to Croydon, and every other small town seeking a glimpse of the new rules of rebellion.

But the interesting point for us to take away is not so much the fact that hip-hop as a music form moved from the margins of popularity to occupy the center and developed into a billion-dollar industry, but that its principles influenced a whole generation of artists to do things differently and to do it themselves.

When RZA formed the Wu-Tang Clan, he had to pay for their studio time with spare change in dollars and cents. Even though they could barely afford to make their first record, "Protect Ya Neck," when the record labels started to smell success, the Wu-Tang Clan refused to abide by the usual industry rules. As the single blew up, label after label approached the crew, but RZA held out as he had one killer condition that no label had seen before and none would agree to. RZA wanted to sign a deal for the Wu-Tang Clan that would allow each member of the crew to also sign as individual artists to any label they liked. RZA was smart enough to know that one label could never back the whole clan as a crew, and support them as individual artists (there were nine of them!), and wanting to make Wu-Tang the biggest-selling hip-hop brand group of all time, he recognized the key to their success would be in insisting their eventual label agree to a clause that once their debut album was released, each crew member could sign up a separate deal with a separate record label. Loud Records shared in RZA's vision to make the Wu-Tang Clan the most successful hip-hop group the world had ever seen and signed them up on RZA's condition.

RZA forced the music industry to rewrite their rules. Once their debut album had gone platinum, he helped each and every one of the rest of the crew to secure a major deal across separate labels, meaning that nine of the world's biggest record companies were all individually investing their resources in pushing the Wu-Tang Clan brand. RZA broke the rules so well, he now had the entire "navy" following his new rules, while his predictions came true and the Wu became the biggest hip-hop artists of all time.

In keeping with his pirate predecessors, RZA laid the foundations of a shared ownership model. Each individual artist's album was always made in partnership with the group, and every release paid into a collective pot, allowing them to start a range of additional enterprises including the multimillion-dollar-earning Wu Wear fashion range. RZA's new rules paid off in millions of dollars for him and the rest of the crew, but they also became the new rules of hip-hop and the dominant idea of artists as enterprises became the norm, or as Jay Z put it when he followed suit, "I'm not a businessman, I'm a business, man."

Hip-hop and its core principles of rebellion and renewal influenced other genres of music, particularly rap. When Chance the Rapper sought advice from his mentor, Childish Gambino, about breaking into the music industry, he decided not to sign a record deal and instead give his mixtape away for free. No threats, no fights, no fuss. Chance flipped conventions and started a mutiny that shook the very heart of the modern music industry. A big statement, but a small act that would make him stand out.

Chance became the first musician to win a Grammy without ever having signed a record deal, for *Coloring Book*, his mixtape that was available free to stream on the internet. He knew that he was taking a risk, but like a pirate, was discovering new ways to find reward. As Chance explained in an interview with *Fader* magazine, he reflected on his pioneering and pirate-like role when he described how the industry looked at him as a pioneer: "They're almost like, 'Keep going. You're in uncharted territory, and you're helping to shed light on what [the future of the business] will look like and we're all curious.'"[11] And in the mind of Chance the Pirate, the risk wasn't so great; from his position at the edges, looking out to the future, the old system obviously held little promise to him, as he told *Rolling Stone* magazine when quizzed on whether he'd ever sign a record deal: "There's no reason to. It's a dead industry."[12]

In his reinvention of the traditional music artist business model, Chance relies on performances, merchandise, and other income streams, meaning his musical choices are his own. The same then becomes true of his political voice. Chance leveraged his fame and reputation unrestrained by the rules of a traditional industry relationship to become an outspoken voice on social issues, and in particular a critic of social justice, welfare, and education.

Chance raised and donated over $1 million to the public school system in Chicago, where he also spontaneously bought an entire neighborhood tickets to the cinema. His achievements prove that rewriting the rules works. He caused good trouble and became a hero and role model to millions in the process. His rebellious actions illustrated to a whole generation that they could do it alone, sending shivers up the timbers of much of the music industry, who rely on convincing future talent they're better off signing contracts and handing over control.

With control on his side, it does look like Chance has done one major deal, in that his next mixtape was available exclusively via Apple Music. It's not a record deal per se, and arguably Apple need Chance more than he needs them in the staying cool stakes, but when you're telling Apple what to do, you know your rebel play has gained you real power. Chance has written new rules that prove you can fight for fairness, find your fortune, and have your own say.

From Herc to RZA to Chance, and hundreds of other hip-hop pirates across fifty years of hip-hop, no matter how big it gets, rewriting the rules is as much a part of hip-hop's DNA as the remix is part of the music.

A Very Modern Mutiny

From Musk to the Wu-Tang Clan to Chance the Rapper, so far we've seen some pretty impressive and dauntingly successful modern pirates. You might be thinking that while these pioneers' achievements are inspiring, they are a little unrelatable, because, let's face it, not all of us know how to build a rocket or spit sixteen bars. But if you look closely, you'll see there are rule breakers and rule remakers operating everywhere, fixing, changing, and bettering the problems they see on a daily basis. Like Teresa Shook, Sophie Collard, Ben Jones, and Jon and Tracy Morter. They had exactly the same tools at their disposal as you do right now and they decided to rewrite the rules of the day.

For Sophie and Ben, that day was one summer's night in 2011 when London exploded into riots so unexpected that the police force were stunned and weren't able to do much beyond some damage limitation. For a wild night, angry, frustrated, and dispossessed people ran the streets, smashing shop windows, looting, starting fires, and generally causing a royal ruckus.

We're not here for the rioters' story. While their explosion of rage was rebellious, it was neither in the cause of good trouble nor about rewriting any rules and offering a better alternative. Sadly for the troubled young people who got caught up in it, it just got them into worse trouble.

The mutiny I want us to learn from that night was rather a call for community, not an attack on it. As night fell, many London streets were under the control of large crowds and few police seemed to be on hand to help. Even the most sympathetic observers retreated to the sanctuary of their homes. Rolling news showed fire after fire on high street after high street, in the closest thing to anarchy many people had seen in their lifetime.

Amid the head scratching, confusion, and questioning, Sophie Collard, aka @sophontrack, started a mutiny against powerlessness when she sent a tweet creating the now legendary tag #riotcleanup. Ben Jones, or @BenDylan, joined the constructive conspiracy when he picked it up and retweeted it so that it was seen by @danthompson, who already ran a social initiative and knew how to turn this small group of rebels into a movement for which he was eventually rewarded by the prime minister. Within hours, thousands of scared, uncertain, and shocked civilians were convening online and agreeing to meet in the still-smoking streets for an enormous cleanup at dawn. And so while many shop fronts still smoldered, members of the community descended on the streets holding brooms and brushes aloft and set to work, setting a new precedent. Their initiative helped the retailers and small businesses whose livelihoods were dependent on the high streets getting back on their feet again, and the alternative and positive headline was a hugely welcomed relief for the media and the rest of Britain. The cleanup brigade offered alternative help that would usually have been left for the police to deal with and restored the country's confidence in a community.

Sometimes a good idea shared is on the streets by the following dawn. Rewrite rules out in the open for others to find and follow.

Teresa Shook is another mutineer who in the spirit of good trouble rewrote the rules with no more in her toolbox than you have now, if you have a social media account and a grievance to rebel against (of which you should have a whole list by now).

On the night of the US elections in November 2016, Teresa wanted to rebel against the incoming president, Donald Trump, and in particular the revelations that had emerged through the election campaign about his attitudes to women. Teresa, a retired lawyer and grandmother, was so incensed about the misogynistic message she felt Trump was peddling that she used her social media account to suggest a demonstration in Washington on inauguration day—a women's march. As with the #riotcleanup mutiny, Teresa awoke the next day to find over 10,000 people had agreed with her. Several other women who'd made similar calls for a modern mutiny had similar responses, with thousands of women contacting them as well. A conspiracy was formed, and a crew of women gathered and made their individual mutinies into a collective reality. They represented various agendas, networks, and eventually countries, and they overcame all their individual perspectives and time zones to make their mutiny a mass movement.

The Women's March 2017 remains the largest single-day protest the United States has ever seen, and became a global day of protest and advocacy of women's rights around the world as almost every other country followed suit.

While those are two major modern mutinies, Jon and Tracy Morter's less political, less consequential, but no less impressive mutiny might be the most mischievous. In December 2009, Jon and Tracy decided to take on Simon Cowell, the brains behind everything from *America's* (and everywhere else's) *Got Talent*, the architect of One Direction, the evil genius behind *The X Factor*, and more crimes against music than we've time to list here.

Fed up with another year of manufactured plasto-pop from the Syco stable dominating the Christmas charts, the music-loving and mutinous couple launched a social media campaign to challenge the *X Factor* winner for the much-coveted Christmas number one position in the UK record charts, which had been held by Cowell's creations for years.

In a moment of genius, Jon and Tracy chose one of their favorite all-time rebel anthems by Rage Against the Machine,

"Killing in the Name," specifically for its chorus line: "Fuck you, I won't do what you tell me."

At first it looked like an inconceivable task to get enough people to buy a seventeen-year-old song from a non-mainstream rap metal band for it to reach number one at Christmas, but a few weeks later and that year's *X Factor* winner and manufactured cheese manifestation, Joe McElderry, was beaten to the top spot as "Killing in the Name" became the first download-only Christmas chart topper. Tracy said: "It was one of those little silly ideas that make you laugh in your own house. We really love music and remember when we were young and the charts were really exciting. We just thought, wouldn't it be funny if that song got to number one?" Rage guitarist Tom Morello said it had "tapped into the silent majority of the people who are tired of being spoon-fed one schmaltzy ballad after another." In a show of good grace and to join a long history of establishment figures recruiting pirate tactics once they've proven their new rules, Simon Cowell said, "I am genuinely impressed by the campaign they have run. . . . I offered them jobs at my record company. It could be in marketing or perhaps even running the company. I wanted them to come and work for us. I was deadly serious, but they haven't taken me up on the offer."

The consistent power of pirates is in the threat of their rebellion, but the potential of pirates is unlocked when their rule breaking turns into rule making.

Free from the limitations and institutions that say there is only one way and it's our way, pirates have nothing to lose, and therefore everything to gain, from being courageous, creative, adventurous, and imaginative, which in turn creates more compelling ideas for others to take inspiration from.

Pirates revel in escaping the suffocation of old rules to try their own stuff out. If you can recognize the old way has run its course, or the rules you're following have passed their sell-by date, then rather than blindly continue to follow someone else's tired ideas, you become free to pursue a rare opportunity to explore your own theories and invite others to test them out.

And don't worry, rule rewriting can sound like heavy lifting, but you don't have to be the grand architect of an entire new system. Every instance we've looked at shows the essence of the *Be More Pirate* approach to writing new rules. The greatest change comes when there is a tight focus on new, experimental, and ambitious rules, formulated by an individual or small group, that become so powerful they are adapted by or inspire the mainstream. Start small, dream big, and get going—that's how pirates bend, break, and remake the rules.

The greatest crimes in the world are not committed by people breaking the rules but by people following the rules.

—Banksy

In the workshops we run, this second stage is where things really get started. We break into crews and a sense of mutiny begins to fill the room. Making new rules can be complex, but that's not where we start; the first thing to do is get a crew to choose the one rule they collectively most want to break, and then begin the task of remaking it.

In this challenge, we've seen things get pretty heated; crews fight, split, re-form, and commit to actual rule breaking there and then. We find when you really reconnect with that rule you know needs breaking, and actual alternatives begin to emerge, with a crew ready to try to change them, pirates begin to get serious.

So to give you your own taste of the challenge in the sessions, please take a few minutes and use the blank page to answer the following question:

If you could break any rule, what would it be? And how would you remake it?

There's only one thing more stupid than stupid rules, and that's the people who follow them. But it's not always helpful just to go around breaking rules. Being more pirate is about questioning, challenging, bending, testing, and ultimately writing better rules.

You don't need to rewrite every rule; start with one that a simple tweak could make better. Rewriting rules isn't about being anarchic for anarchy's sake, it's about improving the conditions we live in and the codes we live by, and it's the right and responsible thing to do.

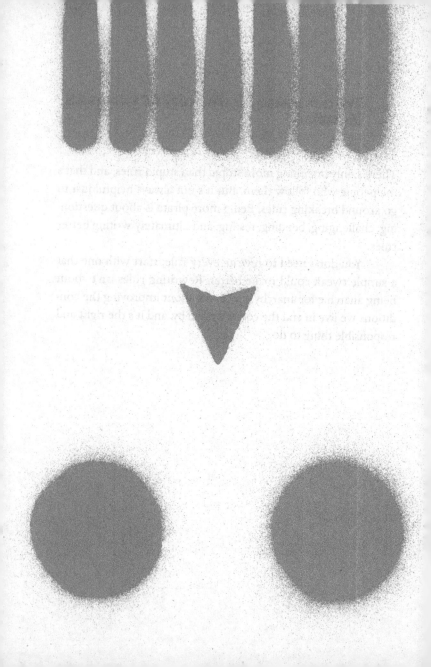

6. REORGANIZE YOURSELF

Or How to Collaborate to Achieve Scale Rather Than Growth

Butterfly Wings in Boxing Gloves

The Golden Age pirates knew that in order to take on far greater odds, build an alternative society, and turn their mutiny into a success, the answer lay in outperforming their rivals, not out-growing them. One core aspect of their power was their ability to organize democratically, and their focus on achieving scale without an accompanying degree of growth that could slow them down and ultimately prove fatal. For the pirates, staying small meant staying strong.

If you want to grow the effectiveness of your mutiny, you need to know how to collaborate within your own small team and then network with other groups of like-minded people without falling prey to the outdated idea that bigger is better. As we saw with the modern examples of piracy at the end of the last chapter, small groups have the ability to ignite big change. The average pirate population during the Golden Age is estimated to have been around 1,500, while the manpower of the Royal Navy topped out at 45,000 before dropping to around 15,000 after the wars against Spain came to an end. The approximate ratio of navy to pirates was therefore 30 to 1 and then later 10 to 1. So how did the pirates stand a chance against an enemy so much larger in size? The main reason they succeeded against such odds was because they embraced the paradox of scale and rejected the static organizing principles of the establishment and replaced them with something much simpler, fairer, more flexible, and more effective.

Of course, it helped that as former employed sailors themselves, they knew exactly where their enemies' vulnerabilities lay. They didn't merely exploit those vulnerabilities, however; they took them as the starting point for their own approach and flipped the old ways on their head. Where their enemies were constrained by ingrained practices and processes, the pirates were agile and deft. Where the establishment was dogmatic and dictatorial, pirates could act both autonomously and collectively, with different crews coming together for a battle and then disbanding again quickly into smaller groups. When the navy tried to overpower them, the pirates used classic David and Goliath tactics to turn the tables. They achieved impressive scale without slowing down; their ability to operate as an agile network is a technique to admire and learn a huge amount from.

Today it's especially important to understand how to collaborate effectively and achieve scale without growth because the idea that we should relentlessly pursue growth is now often stalling our progress and reducing our autonomy. Whether it's bloated government, vast multinational corporations, or the process, people, and politics between you and the person you actually need to talk to, the organizations running our lives are so obese that any notion of accountability or responsiveness has been lost. "Bigger is better" has been an underlying mantra of globalized capitalism, but the problem is, in order for services, goods, supply chains, burgers, download speeds, and shopping malls to constantly get bigger, faster, and shinier, we need to feed consistent economic growth. We've ended up believing that our economies can keep going only if they keep growing. Or as Frederic Laloux, the author of *Reinventing Organizations*, puts it: "We have reached a stage where we often pursue growth for growth's sake, a condition that in medical terminology would simply be called cancer."[1]

Our addiction to growth at any cost explains how we've ended up with enormous conglomerates owning so much. For instance, we're in a situation where pretty much every major food brand in the whole world can be traced up to one of just ten companies. You know most of their names; Mondelēz (Kraft), Nestlé, Mars, PepsiCo, Coca-Cola, etc. And what a reassuring lineup of names it is, too. Thank goodness the life force of humanity is in those loving hands, undoubtedly striving to reduce their environmental impact in line with the planet's needs, respecting cultures and identities with their advertising, producing ever healthier goods, while protecting workers' rights, even if it is occasionally at the cost of their shareholders' returns.

Ahem.

The idea that bigger is better doesn't extend only to physical goods but to online platforms where digital giants obsess over size in an unhealthy way. One of Google's mantras is to "10×" anything they can lay their primary-colored hands on, and Facebook's internal rallying cry is to "move fast and break things" to help them maintain the pace of their incredible growth. Both companies are involved in global infrastructure projects to spread internet connectivity to every corner of the world. Even if it means they have to hang super-enormous hot air balloons carrying powerful internet routers over the world's few remaining Wi-Fi-free zones (which it seems it does), they are on it. I acknowledge that at many levels in all of those organizations there is someone with a sincere agenda to develop solutions to pressing global issues, but even if they are well intended, their overall growth agenda remains problematic. As people wrestle with what they want versus what they really need versus how much the earth can provide, the default assumption that big is good and bigger is better presents an ever-increasing threat.

Om Malik, a venture capitalist with an insight into Silicon Valley, was quoted in 2017 as saying:

> The big companies have been so obsessed with growth that there's been a lack of social responsibility. Now the chickens are coming home to roost. Silicon Valley is very good at using words like empathy as marketing buzz-words, but they are terms we need to internalise as an industry and show through our actions by building the right things. Otherwise it's all bullshit.[2]

It's easy to feel powerless when it seems that a handful of giants exist only to serve their own narrow interests, and it's hard to believe that a small group of people can change things themselves, but the idea that small groups can't change stuff is just not true. Organizational behaviorist Margaret Wheatley expressed this opinion like a pirate when she said:

Despite current ads and slogans, the world doesn't change one person at a time. It changes when networks of relationships form amongst people who share a common cause and vision of what's possible. This is good news for those of us intent on creating a positive future. Rather than worry about critical mass, our work is to foster critical connections. We don't need to convince large numbers of people to change; instead, we need to connect with kindred spirits. Through these relationships, we will develop the new knowledge, practices, courage and commitment that lead to broad-based change.[3]

In other words, ditch the inferiority complex and believe that if you start small and then secure deep engagement from your crew, open collaboration will help you change whatever it is you have in your pirate sights. Even if that's the giants of technology who define the current landscape.

And to cement the point, it might just be that once again, as it was for the pirates, bigger really is no longer better, and the paradox of scale is still on our side. In his excellent essay "The Paradox of Scale," Pete Maulik, managing partner of global innovation agency Fahrenheit 212, argues that now "the world favours the underdog." He warns that for big business "big" is now part of their problem, now that their scale has transformed from "asset" to "liability." And he emboldens the upstarts out there stealing the show, to whom, he argues, power has "irrevocably shifted," using new agile tools to get equal share that previously only a global infrastructure could allow. Pete makes a clear case that power really has shifted.[4]

Malik, Wheatley, and Maulik's arguments that even the biggest institutions are vulnerable to the will of the people is now being proven in the courts of public opinion—for Google and Facebook, at least, who've both seen their brands go rapidly from being loved to turning toxic as a result of those organizations' perceived arrogance.

At the end of the last chapter about rewriting the rules we caught a glimpse of how mutinies had the potential to turn into movements overnight. In this chapter, we'll see how pirates turn their mutinies into well-structured communities who prize collaboration and connection above all else. If you reorganize like pirates, there's no need to keep growing just to keep going.

Pirate Ships Were Fairer and More Diverse Than Anywhere You've Ever Worked

Before we began this section of our reeducation of pirates, most of us probably assumed that pirate crews were anarchic, chaotic, and drunken. Well, most of us would be wrong. In truth, pirate ships were exceptionally well run, equitable, and accountable, though they were indeed drunken from time to time.

Many pirates had experienced both the brutality and the best training of either the Royal or Merchant Navy. They took the skills, techniques, and tactics these organizations taught them but resented and rejected the exploitation, bullying, and hierarchy that was also on offer. Other pirates came in the form of freed or escaped slaves who'd experienced humanity at its most inhuman. Organization aboard pirate ships was designed to rectify the poor conditions both groups had endured. The pirates came up with new rules and systems to prevent anyone from being similarly mistreated. Of course, crew members all hoped for a lucrative income, but pirate ships were also designed to provide a fairer way of life where members would get not only equal pay but also an equal say.

Pirates designed democratic structures that predated the English, French, and American systems of representative democracy, which, as we've discussed, were more participatory than anything that even the good old Greeks managed back in ancient Athens, where suffrage didn't extend beyond an elite group of white males. Pirate democracy usually included everyone. On pirate ships, and eventually in the Republic of Pirates, the policy was one pirate, one vote on most matters.

And it doesn't stop there. Democracy is great in theory but can be clumsy in practice—all groups need a system of governance in order to operate effectively, especially when under threat. Pirates knew instinctively and ahead of their time that nothing sucks more than an org chart. (If you aren't familiar with the term, then lucky you. Basically, an org chart is an always-out-of-date family tree for an office, often a Human Resources person's equivalent of a meth habit.) To avoid implementing a painful hierarchy or a chain of command that could be abused, the pirates invented a responsive way of organizing themselves that allowed order to be maintained when they were in need of cohesive leadership. If the pirates were under attack or busy taking a "prize," the captain temporarily became the all-powerful commander, but as soon as the engagement was over, democracy reigned once again.

This dynamism and an almost instinctual ability to shift between a type of organizational collectivism and total authoritarianism look to me a lot like an early form of the Holacracy movement. Holacracy is a modern form of nonhierarchical but dynamic management "invented" in 2007 that predicts the future will be "self-organizing." Many managers in mainstream organizations may find it a little ahead of its time (in other words, terrifying), but it's worth investigating, because if the pirates' track record is anything to go by, its day will come. Holacracy sounds like a very twenty-first-century concept, but the idea of setting your own rules is as old as the eighteenth-century pirates, and just as every pirate prediction eventually ended up influencing the mainstream, self-organization is likely to follow.

Beyond one-pirate, one-vote proto-democracy and an agile organizing principle that could switch between quasi-socialism and a temporary dictatorship in times of conflict, pirates also instinctively knew that nothing makes a good team great as effectively as ensuring it's a diverse one.

The broad reach of their recruiting meant that the pirates had a phenomenal pool of talent at their disposal. Their blindness to color and focus on talent resulted in some significant nonwhite leaders emerging in the Golden Age. Black Caesar, a tribal chief who had been kidnapped from Africa and escaped from slavery, was welcomed into the pirate brethren as leader, strategist, and man of great strength, eventually becoming Blackbeard's right-hand man and a renowned pirate captain in his own right. Pirates weren't proactively progressive, but even if as a by-product of a talent-first approach to recruitment, by today's standards it's still ahead of the curve.

Indeed, it could be argued that the pirates of the Golden Age were among the world's first equal opportunity employers. Admittedly, the turn of the eighteenth century isn't famous for fairness to marginal groups, but history is on the side of the pirates here, and if you're skeptical, remember Anne Bonny and Mary Read, proto-feminists who were accepted and respected on deck. The same was true for ethnic minority crew members and same-sex couples. "The deck of a pirate ship was the most empowering place for blacks within the eighteenth-century white man's world,"[5] said Kenneth Kinkor when he was project historian at Expedition Whydah, an organization on Cape Cod whose museum houses artifacts from the first documented pirate shipwreck ever recovered. In his essay "Black Men Under the Black Flag," Kinkor counted nonwhite crew members under piracy's most influential captains: Samuel Bellamy 27 out of 180, Edward England 50 out of 180, and Blackbeard 60 out of 100. Across all pirate ships, nonwhite crew members averaged out to around 33 percent.[6] Just for reference, that would make an eye-wateringly ambitious diversity target for many of the twenty-first century's most progressive major employers. Global bean-counting and consultancy firm Pricewaterhouse-Coopers, who are leaders in the field, have a global target of 25 percent diversity, among a "global" team.

We've already touched on the stories and significance of some of the legendary female pirates. And there are others such as Jacquotte Delahaye and Grace O'Malley who are also very visible in broader pirate history, but a much less well known part of pirates' progressive attitudes was their recognition of gay rights. A degree of homosexuality was common at sea as things got pretty close between the men after many months aboard. In the navies, the same was also true, but was very severely punished, giving rise to the infamous Winston Churchill quote, where he summarized the values of the Royal Navy as "rum, sodomy, and the lash." As we're learning, the norm on pirate ships was a wholescale rejection of the repression of navy life. Pirates recognized that deep and meaningful relationships evolved between crew members, and instead of punishing them, they literally celebrated them. Pirate society took same-sex relationships so seriously that they created rituals and legal practices around them. They gave the name "matelotage" to the deep bonds between men, sometimes even with a ceremony attached, and the happy couple could signify their willingness to share rights of ownership and inheritance if they so chose. Again, these principles were not intentionally progressive, and there's much debate about how widely used they were, but in at least some instances, for purely practical reasons, pirate crews sometimes included what would now be seen as openly gay elements and practised a form of same-sex marriage.

So, even if it was more by default than design, pirates created an organizational model with an environment that was very, very far ahead of the times: diverse and highly responsive to both its members' talents and their needs and sensitive to the harsh realities of conflict. . . . As a result they were a tight and loyal bunch who pooled all their resources to share rewards, risks, and decision-making. Impressive, interesting, inspiring—but what are the key lessons in there for you?

Try doubling down on these points. First, pirates created inclusive systems of organization that fostered strong bonds between diverse crew members, making them accountable to one another and innovative in their thinking. They practiced equality, but they were tough about talent—they didn't carry dead weight or suffer fools, they saw talent before color, gender, or age, and most important, they acknowledged the benefit of a diversity of backgrounds.

You can do exactly the same; if you apply the same blend of principle and pragmatism as the pirates, there is no limit to the talent you can surround yourself with. The more open you are toward deliberate diversity, the more innovation will follow. The more vigorously you encourage collaboration and connection between those diverse elements rather than defaulting to one single opinion, the better. There is no single organizational model you are obliged to follow. There is no one type of person you or your team should strive to imitate (and if you do all look the same, then something's gone wrong). When it comes to diversity, ethnicity and gender aren't the only important elements. Surround yourself with people who also think differently from you and you're sure to stay ahead.

Pirates Were Agile Before Agile Was a Thing

Operating in nonhierarchical and accountable teams that valued diversity of skills and opinions gave pirates an edge over their foes and competitors. The other main weapon in their organizational arsenal was the ability to respond fast to a dynamic situation. As we've seen, part of this was the ability to switch between a collective decision-making model and a hierarchical one with a single authority figure before (crucially) reverting back to the collective. But the other incredible facet of pirates' organizational responsiveness was less about leadership and more about a willingness to assemble and then disband teams as the situation demanded. Pirates scaled up their crew when they needed to and scaled down again afterward which meant there was always just enough skill and labor to take on a challenge, whatever its dimensions.

According to statistics from pirate historian Marcus Rediker, the average size of a pirate crew was around eighty men.[7] Blackbeard was in command of just twenty men on one ship when he was caught and killed, though he's known to have commanded hundreds of men across vast fleets at points in his career. On one of his missions he amassed such a flotilla and caused so much mischief along the eastern seaboard that he was able to hold the entire coastal city of Charleston, South Carolina, hostage for a week, an act of such military, political, and economic significance that it led to the "1718 pirate crisis," as it was known, that swept North America that summer.

One of the largest pirate crews ever assembled was organized by Henry Morgan, who put out the Call of the Brethren across the New World and united crews from all countries and cultures for an all-out assault on Panama City, a strategic outpost of the Spanish empire. Bringing together 2,000 men, Morgan shamelessly, savagely, but successfully looted the city in one of his most infamous misadventures whose ramifications would be felt all the way to the early establishment of the British empire. Once the city was in ashes, the pirates crewed down with as much ease as they had teamed up, demonstrating the incredible dynamic force, responsiveness, and flexibility of their ability at networked organization.

Though they may have used their might for dubious purpose, their ability to scale up and down from the nimblest of twenty-person teams to the city-shattering strength of two thousand is admirable even by today's "agile first" standards. Operating at different capacities, blending teams of people from different cultures with diverse capabilities to create devastating results would be impressive now, let alone three centuries ago.

Today there's a lot of lip service paid to the notion of staying nimble, but it's often undercut by a ton of bureaucracy that seems unshiftable. On the other hand, sometimes "stay nimble" simply operates as a euphemism for "regulation slows us down and we must get rid of it so we're free to exploit workers and resources as we see fit." The Golden Age pirates show us something different. Their ability to achieve scale through collaboration is one of the most important lessons I believe they have to teach for our twenty-first-century adventures. And in our day and age, when digital networks offer limitless opportunity to crew up, band together, or mutate, we have infinitely more ways to join our small groups together, find inspiration or best practice, gather more people, push for more access, and create more change quicker.

Problems Become Solutions for Pirates

There are hundreds if not thousands of groups all around the world experimenting in politics and activism, fundraising, retail, and any other field you can think of, who are reorganizing themselves in a pirate-like way today.

In 2012 the Taiwanese government infuriated its people by telling them not to "waste time talking about their policies" and the economic plan but instead get on with their daily toil, which would supposedly benefit the economy from the bottom up. This patronizing political pat on the head for a population who had enjoyed democracy for only a few generations was one step too far for a group of young computer programmers who decided to go pirate and began a smart underground tech-enabled rebellion that sparked Taiwan's Sunflower Revolution. This group flipped the sluggish and out-of-date ruling power on its head by "forking" it. They created parallel "forked" websites for key government institutions and made their pretend sites more convincing, more compelling, and ultimately more collaborative than the real ones, and in the process engaged hundreds of thousands of citizens, who arrived online to prove exactly how civic participation in public decision-making could operate if only you were serious about wanting it to happen. The Sunflower Revolution sparked a change in attitude and led to a different model of democracy being implemented in Taiwan. From the Accounting and Statistics Office running participatory budgeting processes to a mass civic deliberation on how to respond to the arrival of Uber, today Taiwan is at the forefront of a very different model of democracy as a result of getting "forked." In 2018 it was ranked the most open government in the world at 90 percent by the Global Open Data Index.[8] (The UK is joint second with Australia at 79 percent, USA is joint eleventh with Mexico at 65 percent.) The small group of

Taiwanese students who organized a digital coup caused good trouble and changed mainstream ideals for the better—one of the pioneers who set up the "forks," Audrey Tang, now works on the inside as digital minister for Taiwan, the country's first transgender minister. Taiwan's digital and democratic pirates started something extraordinary, but they aren't the only group of people looking to shake up politics and pull the rug from under the myth that only top-down scale, command-and-control, growth-or-die strategies are effective in politics or civic administration. Portugal created the world's first national-scale participatory budgeting process and France wasn't far behind, assigning over €100 million of government spending each year through deliberative digital democracy. In Iceland, nearly half the population have participated in an online democracy platform since 2011, and the small Andalusian town of Jun's citizens govern themselves almost entirely through Twitter. Even Mexico City, which has one of the biggest metropolitan populaces on earth, began to crowdsource its constitution in 2016 through change.org.

So far, so empowering, and so apparent that the tools of rebellion are available to us all. It's been proven beyond a doubt that all over the world a pirate approach to reorganization coupled with clever use of technology can wrench power from the establishment and place it in the hands of the people. But it's not just self-interested governments that pirate principles applied to modern movements have been teaching a lesson.

In 2015, we realized that the world's largest taxi firm, Uber, owns no cars; the world's most popular media company, Facebook, creates no content; the world's most valuable retailer,

Alibaba, carries no stock; and the world's largest accommodation provider, Airbnb, owns no property. It was actually internationally renowned marketing guru Tom Goodwin who first made this observation, since when the rest of the world has repeated it (and taken the credit for it) to each other a million times. Tom further observed that "something big is going on," and he wasn't wrong, although my contribution is that in all these instances, big isn't always better.

Tom disarmingly poked fun at the worldwide acclaim his (often unattributed) insight received when announcing his book *Digital Darwinism: Survival of the Fittest in the Age of Business Disruption*, tweeting: "You hated and are bored by the quote, now come tolerate the book." Lol. (It's actually really good.)

After the initial international excitement that this new "sharing economy" of Airbnb, Uber, TaskRabbit, Deliveroo, and many others promised an enlightened, more community oriented way of doing business had subsided, the age-old accusations of tax avoidance, poor working conditions, and negative impact on disrupted local economies all followed.

The dip in reputation of these new tech-enabled giants on the block followed that of their predecessors Facebook and Google, whose once bright promise that "technology will save us" has perhaps shifted to "technology will make a fortune from our data and then dodge its taxes and avoid responsibility for abuses of its platform," which may or may not be entirely fair, but is increasingly a perspective our potential tech saviors need to overcome.

All of a sudden, Tom's "something big" observation didn't sound quite so beautiful.

Back out at the edges where pirates gather, a movement has started in response to this new evolution of big bad business under the guise of the "gig economy." If history tells us anything, it's that pirate movements in response to unfair systems start by kicking at the edges but often end up becoming mainstream ideas over time.

Defying great odds—famed for flying in the face of unfairness and ultimately encouraging the establishment to adopt their alternative ideas—is the pirate approach to fix an unfair enemy, and based on such a precedent, this could be an interesting conflict to watch. There are certainly some pirates beginning to gather in formation for this particular fight; they fly under a flag called platform cooperativism, and it's pirate to its core.

This is how the movement describes itself: Platform cooperativism is a growing international movement that builds a fairer future of work. It's about social justice and the bottom line. Rooted in democratic ownership, co-op members, technologists, unionists, and freelancers create a concrete near-future alternative to the extractive sharing economy.

Making good on the early promise of the Web to decentralize the power of apps, protocols, and websites, platform co-ops allow households with low and volatile income to benefit from the shift of labor markets to the Internet. Steering clear of the belief in one-click fixes of social problems, the model is poised to vitalize people-centered innovation by joining the rich heritage and values of co-ops with emerging Internet technologies.[9]

Consider all the new big businesses we can't imagine life without. I'm talking Amazon, Uber, eBay, etc. Then take a look at the rapidly growing platform cooperative movement and you'll be surprised to see that the apps you begrudgingly depend on for food delivery, car sharing, taxi hailing, housecleaning, stuff buying, old-stuff auctioning, social networking, and so on are all there in some form but reimagined, reorganized, and made fair.

There's a growing directory of platform cooperatives operating in most major markets. They're definitely in their pirate stage—small, at the fringes, innovating, rebelling, and rewriting rules—but they organize themselves and their power is growing. FairBnB does what the name suggests, providing an Airbnb alternative that's owned by its users and paying a fair share to renters.

If you ever sympathized with #deleteuber but couldn't bear to lose the convenience of the world's biggest ride-hailing app, many major cities have a driver-owned alternative to Uber, from Alpha Taxis in Paris to Co-op Cabs in Toronto. And as ever, because the pirates are exploring new ways of organizing at the edges, there's innovation and imagination on fire, with multiple Blockchain-powered platforms, others pushing the boundaries of property ownership, freelancers' support systems adapting to the changing world of work, and many more. As history shows, pirates have a tendency to accurately predict future trends, and the platform co-op directory to me feels like a glimpse into that future.

The platform co-op people introduce themselves eloquently: "The Internet *can* be owned and governed differently.

The experiments now already underway show that a global ecosystem of cooperatives and unions, in collaboration with movements such as Free and Open Source Software, can stand against the concentration of wealth and the insecurity of workers that yields Silicon Valley's winner-takes-all economy."[10]

I doubt even pirate captain "Black" Sam Bellamy, the rabble-rousing orator, could have said it better. If we've learned anything from pirate history so far, it's that their ideas are over time adopted by the mainstream, and therefore platforms such as these are ones to watch. My bet is that some of these cooperative-based apps are the platforms and marketplaces of the future, the next iteration, and hopefully with their principles of fairness maintained while they also make their fortune.

In 2016, the idea that someone could take Facebook's crown seemed unthinkably naive. Just a few years later, its reputation in toxic tatters, the promise of the platform cooperatives seems more in the ascendance than ever.

There are literally hundreds of thousands of small groups of people out there pushing their mini-mutinies, determined to cause big change. Whether they start as a WhatsApp group or in a bar, an office, or a communal working space doesn't matter. A mutiny can be a beautiful thing where it allows fairness, creativity, and change to flourish. At some point, though, if you want to continue to crew up and find the modern version of Henry Morgan's Call of the Brethren that brings thousands of pirates together to make the whole world listen, you'll need to turn your mutiny into a networked movement, which these days means turning technology to your advantage.

How to Turn a Mutiny into a Movement

One particularly inspiring and accessible example of a small team creating multiple mutinies influencing millions of people is Avaaz. Avaaz, meaning "voice," as in what it gives to multiple issues every day, is a network of modern-day pirates with world-changing ideas of systems-level change. The *Guardian* newspaper describes them as "the globe's largest and most powerful online activist network."[11] In his role as environmental campaigner, ex-vice-president Al Gore has called them "inspiring," and multiple government records released to the public reveal that ministers fear them. But Avaaz has also been accused of embodying Slacktivism, allowing people to cop out of real decision-making. So what is it, and who is behind it?

Avaaz calls itself a "campaigning community" that uses the internet to bring together its tens of millions of members to debate, decide, choose, and lead its campaigns. Its goals range from liberating journalists in oppressive regimes to protecting endangered species and much, much more besides.

Avaaz was launched in 2007 by a consortium of experienced watchmen of social injustice. It's led by Ricken Patel, an accomplished expert in rebels, conflicts, and corrupt systems who understands how to use the levers of power, politics, and technology to manipulate and manage them all. Avaaz brings together a small but diverse team of highly skilled and talented people from all over the world and sets out to build a highly sophisticated digital platform that makes participation very easy. The concept is simple and speaks directly to what Margaret

Wheatley told us was the way to build significant change in the twenty-first century. Don't aim for big, aim for connected. Find or build a community of other people who care about the same things you do and act together to lobby, protest, and insist.

With a massive membership in the tens of millions and a tiny core team, Avaaz routinely takes on seemingly insurmountable challenges and very often wins. By wielding the power of its network it often leaves rivals with two black eyes. In its own words: "From technology [comes] new nimbleness and flexibility. . . . Instead of fragmenting, we grow—united by values."[12] It is mighty on an international scale, but nimble and efficient, meaning its campaigning power is "always on," far beyond the influence of ordinary four-yearly election cycles. And talking of politics, Avaaz takes on all comers, from presidents to corrupt systems and major corporations. And all three, when they happen to be the same thing. Refusing any income from political parties or big business, it relies on small donations from its member base. From mobilizing the largest ever demonstration against climate change to rallying against some of the world's least favorite businesses and their evil supervillain leaders, from Monsanto to Murdoch, while championing the rights of marine life, bees, and refugees along the way, Avaaz backs the underdog, fights for what's right, wins court cases, gets policy changed, and influences the influencers.

As a demonstration of the pirate principle that nimble networks can collaborate to create scale with a strength to take on superpowers, the story speaks for itself. Currently Avaaz is running global campaigns with a team whose members are based in over thirty countries, using all available technology platforms to organize efficiently. Campaign ideas come from its millions of subscribers and are then shaped by a small team of experts. Ideas are refined extensively using agile techniques within a bespoke responsive testing community of 10,000 representative members. But they are not limited to digital campaigning, and often create real-world and physical events, such as a three-mile human handshake organized by the Dalai Lama from the Royal Albert Hall to the doors of the Chinese embassy in London, to represent and request both sides engage more meaningfully with one another.

If you want to test-drive a monumental collaborative tool without taking the risk of leaving your house, just sign up to Avaaz; search the fights they are having on behalf of humanity and add your name to those you believe in. Watch the updates, subscribe to the social feeds, and see how they leverage change. You'll get a sense of how a modern-day pirate-like network works alongside 44 million other crew members. If you really want to see how powerfully pirate Avaaz can be, start a campaign yourself. It's free and incredibly quick, and puts you in touch with crew members like yourself who are amassing global communities against deforestation, restrictive internet freedoms, political corruption, or the commercial development of local public spaces. At the very least, try joining someone else's crew or campaign for a while and take inspiration as you join in a fight you'd probably never be able to win alone. Avaaz really stacks up as an exemplary pirate organizer.

Its political- and social-activist platforms are predicated on staying small as a team and taking direction from members on matters of policy, crewing up as necessary to take on the world's biggest challenges through an agile network. The organization has been built on the founding pirate principles of the two previous chapters. Patel and his followers are fearless rebels when it comes to defying corporations and corrupt politicians. They rewrote the rule that insisted online petitions were a waste of time. They have inspired many more platforms to follow them. They may not be perfect, and many would argue they're far from it, but I'm convinced they indicate a new way of engaging with issues that's here to stay and that will grow. The idea of platforms like these, the technology they're based on using, the victories they've begun to win—all of it is just at the beginning of their potential. As Avaaz and the other platforms doing very similar work evolve and, like pirates, continue to influence the mainstream, it's surely a safe bet that this sort of platform participation in politics and society is going to become more and more prevalent. Avaaz's work is governed by pirate principles playing out three hundred years on, standing up to the same sorts of unfair systems, dodgy big business, and untrustworthy leaders, while giving voice to those who don't have one. The similarities seem clear, the lessons look valuable. No shortage of world leaders are on record as taking notice. National letdown and former prime minister of the UK Gordon Brown said, "Avaaz has driven forward the idealism of the world . . . do not underestimate your impact on leaders . . . you rascally wee pirates." Okay, so he didn't say the very last bit, but the rest is true.

Dead Ahead

You're now bristling with examples of how pirates both vintage and contemporary have grown their mutinies into movements, harnessed the power of small groups, and crewed up and down as required through the power of networks. The Golden Age pirates turned the navy's way of organizing on its head and in the process invented extraordinarily responsive, agile, and nimble structures long before such buzzwords were even dreamt of, let alone considered best practice. Starting from the principle that says big is no longer better and small groups are powerful, even more so when they network, we've looked at how you can reorganize yourself from the outset to create radical change, not cancerous growth.

If we're going to ride the stormy seas ahead, we need all the pointers we can get. Change and challenge are constants, and the way we organize ourselves to meet them is going to be crucial as we navigate the twenty-first century. The skills we need to do so are going to look increasingly different, too.

In our accelerating world, the other end of the argument that we need to organize ourselves differently is not just about the best way of operating at a macro scale, it's also about the micro scale. In particular the optimum size of organizations, and how it appears to be shrinking.

In 1965, Standard & Poor's index of American businesses registered that the average life expectancy of firms was sixty-five years. Fifty years later, in 2015, this had dropped to a fifteen-year average life expectancy. If the trend continues in even the crudest way, then by 2025 the lifetime of the average company could hit somewhere near five years.

The flip side of that statistic is the rapid increase in business birthrates. Taking the UK this time as a proxy, but following the same time frame, from the 1960s to 2015, the volume of operating businesses rose from 750,000 to over 5 million. By 2025, on a similar trajectory, we'll be looking at 7 million, or one business for every ten people.

The US and the UK are fairly reliable proxies for what seems to be a global trend, where it's clear that in the coming years, many more organizations will exist for much shorter periods of time, making the importance of collaboration and networks to achieve solutions at scale increasingly important.

We're all set for faster, bolder, shorter adventures. Where once there was hierarchical structure, a long slow climb up the career ladder, a culture of internal competition combined with deference to remote leaders, bureaucracy, and that's-just-how-it-is attitudes, there will now be collaborative skills, responsive mechanisms, and shared principles to live and die by. Described like that, the future sure sounds a lot like the true history of the Golden Age of pirates.

They paint the world full of shadows and then tell their children to stay close to the light.... But in the dark, there is discovery, there is possibility, there is freedom.

—Captain Flint

Reorganization can be complex. In this chapter I've shown the simple but sophisticated systems pirates used to organize themselves and take on the world successfully.

Today the idea that bigger is better is losing ground fast, and once again agility, instinct, and the right individuals can overcome even the greatest odds.

Having covered the power of networks, the paradox of scale, the tyranny of growth, and ultimately, the idea that all it takes to change the world is a committed group of thoughtful citizens, give yourself a few minutes to consider this question:

Who out there would you most like to take down?

Not take out, but take down, perhaps a peg or two, perhaps more. Who are the biggest possible rivals who have similar ideas or the same ambition? Whose crown would you like to see slip?

Who is your navy, pirate?

In workshops, this challenge usually initiates an excited listing exercise, so make a note of as many as you want, but aim for a short list of three to five targets. Remain open as to who can be on there: individuals, institutions, organizations, platforms, or businesses.

And don't hold back; be brave, be ambitious, be imaginative, be unrealistic. If it's the huge tech player that's disrupted your whole industry, remember they were the disrupter once, and the next disrupter after them is actually their greatest fear. If it's the people doing your idea, only faster and with more resources and less baggage, then watch, learn, and bide your time. If it's the hundred-year-old institution that shows no sign of moving, remember what happens to dinosaurs.

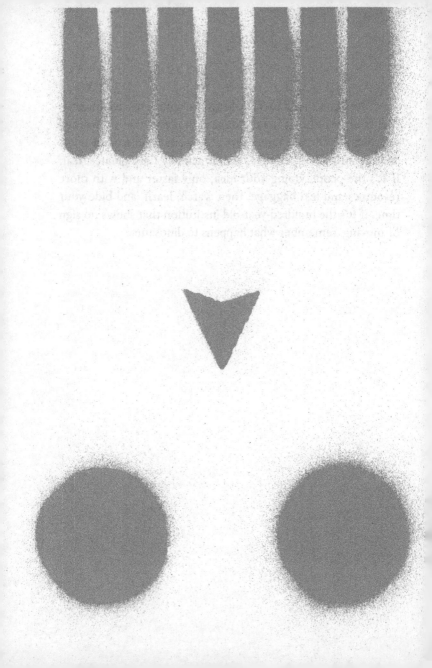

7. REDISTRIBUTE POWER

Or How to Fight for Fairness and Make Enemies of Exploitation

Fierce Fairness

We're reaching a crucial stage in your pirate journey. Hopefully you already know the mutiny you'd like to begin; hopefully you're gathering a crew, energy, and conviction as you start to believe that you can find new solutions to approach old problems. If you can see change on the horizon, then you might already be feeling a rush of excitement. I hope so. If you haven't got started yet, have no fear, the pirate change framework comes with a rush-of-excitement guarantee; once you begin to put the first stages into practice, you will feel it. But there are some new challenges that come with these early wins. Once your rebellion is a success, no matter how small; once your new rules are being followed, even if it's only by one person; once you're collaborating, not growing; once you've felt the power that comes from creating change, what are you going to do with it, and how are you going to protect it?

Will you continue to champion the change you've caused with unwavering integrity, or will you disappointingly but predictably dilute that difference you wanted to make by succumbing to side deals and compromising your principles to cling on to power?

It's the implementation of this penultimate of the five pirate principles, the redistribution of power, that will determine whether the change you're working for will hold true or get blown off course. Each stage is important, but in this chapter we learn how to start to protect all that's gone before as we see the potency of handing over power, sharing profit, and opening up decision-making to preserve our integrity. Any upstart or egotist can rebel, rewrite, and reorganize themselves around a cause for all sorts of morally ambiguous reasons, and that's what makes this step so important; there are many alt-disrupters and ideologues who might appear to be following the first three pirate principles, but what separates us and them is taking the next step to redistribute power and make an enemy of exploitation. If you ensure part of your rebellion is to redistribute power and fight for fairness, you protect the cause of good trouble, not just trouble in and of itself.

Power makes a Gollum out of most of us in the end. There's a reason that revolutions turn into institutions, and heroes who fought for freedom give way to and often become part of disappointingly corrupt administrations. Nothing will be different this time unless we set out to share our power differently. The pirates learned this the hard way and saw it in pretty stark terms: redistributing power is the way to protect the integrity of our change and maintain respect for one another in the process. There was no way the Golden Age pirates were going to fight so hard for a different way of doing things only to let the bad habits of exploitative muggles creep back in, so they designed processes that *forced* fairness. You can't grow a mutiny into a movement, organize yourself to react quickly to challenges, or achieve great things if you insist on clinging to old top-down lines of command. We like to think we can, but history tells us again and again we can't. Ask the Zapatistas, Che Guevara, Nelson Mandela, or a long list of freedom fighters turned politicians if they're pleased with how their revolutions turned out. It's very hard to play nice with power. The pirates protected what they had built from corruption, ego, and greed by getting militantly strict about fairness. But make no mistake, they didn't just get all "sharing is caring" because of a dedication to social responsibility; they knew that clear principles could protect what they'd fought for and give them an advantage.

If you are going to overcome the challenge in front of you, start that thing you've been thinking about starting, and take on the world, you will go far further if you view establishing your principles as your foundation. And please, don't make the mistake that too many people do when they hear words like "principles" and "fairness"—that this is the "fluffy" section that can be skipped. That would be as grave a mistake as believing that those emblazoning their walls, sweat shirts, and Instagram accounts with "fluffy" statements really live by them. I am always a bit suspicious that those who feel they need to remind others to "work hard and be nice to people" are covering up their own inner difficulty in doing just that.

Instead, I suspect the pirate approach was more of a mutual assumption that everyone agrees not to be a pain in the ass as the collective baseline, and from there, sincerely held values and principles become a defining competitive edge. It's about deciding what is important, what is your North Star when you're lost, what is the currency with which you collaborate and negotiate, and where the bottom line that protects your authenticity and integrity is drawn. The pirates had this under control—they had to. They were outlaws who had to trust one another implicitly and understand one another's motivation because their collective survival depended on it. They designed precise mechanisms to make their power equitable and minimize the obvious opportunities for conflict that they'd hated under a command-and-control setting in the navy. They lived by the maxim "No prey, no pay," which meant that every pirate should receive a fair (and in most cases equal) share of everything they stole. They invented workplace injury compensation hundreds of years before any industry caught on and they administered everything relating to money, as well as duties and responsibilities, with complete transparency. Sure, they wanted to be paid fairly (and hopefully fantastically from all that stolen treasure), but they also wanted to be treated equally and participate fully in the decision-making that ran the ship. So they pioneered universal suffrage, elected leaders, and came up with a dual-governance leadership structure. Essentially, they valued equality and were prepared to share power in order to achieve and protect it.

Peter Leeson, author of *The Invisible Hook*, provides a rational economic perspective that may explain their seemingly innovative stance:

> Pirates needed to avoid as many opportunities for violent conflict that could erupt into fighting and tear the organization apart. Unsurprisingly the greatest divisive force that

threatened this possibility was money. To minimize the chance of natural human emotions disrupting or even totally undermining their profit-making purpose, pirates eliminated the greatest potential source of these emotions, large material inequalities.[1]

Pirates did not "do good" for the sake of doing good. They were not trying to clumsily "give back," or racked by the existential "purpose" crises many individuals and organizations find themselves in circular conversations around today. Yet they held an approach that could benefit anyone facing that conundrum. They knew what they wanted, they knew what they stood for, and they established principles so profound they could rely on them to inform their strategy even in the middle of a fight and amid the uncertainty of their times.

Pioneers of Power-Sharing

We've already looked at the one-pirate, one-vote model of democracy, but the pirates protected the shared sense of power by going even further, at times allowing captains to be voted in or out by the crew, making their democratic power fully accountable to the people. In *The Invisible Hook*, Leeson states:

It is truly remarkable to think that this model of democracy was staged not only on a pirate ship, of all places, but took place more than half a century before the Continental Congress approved the Declaration of Independence and only a little more than a decade after the British monarchy withheld Royal Assent for the last time. Pirate democracy extended the unrestricted right to pirates to have a say in the selection of their society's leaders nearly 150 years before the Second Reform Act of 1868 accomplished anything close to the same in Britain.[2]

The pirates pioneered an early form of democracy that championed universal suffrage and the election of the people's leader by the people, but they also had a unique approach to leadership once a captain was in place. The pirates embraced a system of dual governance whereby the quartermaster was granted power equal to that of the captain. Under dual governance, the quartermaster was the voice of the crew and culture while the captain led the strategy. So far, very modern management principles.

Just as they handled leadership democratically, pirates had an equally forward-thinking approach to handling income, pay, and profit. In the navy, you could sail the seven seas many times over, but you might not get paid for it. Pay was infrequent, at the mercy of tyrannical and sometimes thieving captains, and occasionally didn't happen at all or was replaced by a token system. Indentured or press-ganged men were forced, kidnapped, tricked, or even drugged into service without the opportunity to agree on a salary in the first place. Those who had previously been slaves had no income whatsoever. In contrast, pirates paid themselves fairly and squarely. On pirate ships, pay was a sophisticatedly simple and decidedly democratic right, with three main conditions:

1. No plunder, no pay.

If the captain and crew didn't win a prize (i.e., capture and loot a ship), then no one got paid and everyone had to rely on the same rations and reserves to survive. Unlike today, there was certainly no pay for underperforming bosses. Captain, quartermaster, and cabin boy all lived, died, ate, and got paid under the same principle.

2. Open incentives for going beyond the call of duty.

These differed from crew to crew, but were transparent and clear rewards available to all members of the crew. Being the first to spot a ship on the horizon (be it a prize or a predator) could earn that crew member a reward, such as a choice of any weapon won from taking that prize.

3. Fair shares for all crew members.

All surviving records of Pirate Codes indicate a system of proportional pay that saw the vast majority of the crew take an even share of the booty, whether they were freed slaves, women, boys, drunk, or half dead. If they were on the account, they were on the payroll at the same rate as everyone else. Only a handful of senior players like the ship's carpenter, doctor, quartermaster, and captain received a greater but corresponding amount, usually checked somewhere between two and four times larger than the average share. This higher ratio recognized roles of greater responsibility or risk, and it was a transparent transaction that all the crew were aware of and even played a hand in agreeing to.

The progressive ideals about fair compensation aboard pirate ships didn't stop at pay packets. They also extended into injury in the line of duty, creating a system of social insurance approximately two hundred years before it became standardized around the world. Pirates' compensation was calculated on a sliding scale that took into account everything from the loss of a leg to a finger's being chopped off or an eye being gouged out, each event apportioned an appropriate amount. The pirate payout varied surprisingly little from crew to crew and throughout the Golden Age and was universally approximately 800 pieces of gold for a lost leg and 100 pieces of gold for a lost eye, which might sound blunt or even upside down, but it was a lot more sophisticated and fairer than the rest of the working world. The injury compensation scheme was a case of enlightened interest applying collectively across the whole community. There was collective agreement that introducing some payout on injury was the right thing to do, not just for the leadership but for everyone.

The pirates' attitudes to power and pay illustrate the undeniable correlation they recognized between transparency and accountability. They all knew how much they would get paid and how much they would be compensated for any injury they sustained. They also knew how much everyone else would get paid, and they were encouraged to be more accountable by tying together individual and collective reward. It doesn't really need saying, but I will: that level of transparency around pay is not yet something that almost any mainstream business at almost any level does as well as pirates did.

Not to mention those three little words: gender pay gap.

The pirates' enlightened approach to power distribution inspires us to fight for what we deserve and expect: equality, a fair share, reward for risk, and a commitment to avoid exploitation. Pirates had policies concerning all these areas to make success and failure a collective act, a powerful technique to align a team and harness the ideas of fairness, self-direction, and purpose to become wind in your sails.

Their implementation of dual governance and focus on nonhierarchical facilitative leadership are especially important lessons to learn today. As the concept of global leadership fails us to the point that it risks becoming oxymoronic, the next generation no longer look upward for inspiration or wait for power to be handed down to them, nor should they.

Leadership and knowledge sharing were once always top-down concepts, but they're shifting to a horizontal perspective, as the leadership role models of today are more likely to be peers that you can access than figureheads who seem so far out of reach and out of touch. If you're seeking someone to look up to in the twenty-first century, instead look sideways at your peers and inwards at yourself, because there's an absence of inspiring and progressive leadership up ahead.

In mainstream business leadership, original thought and the promise of power-sharing seem, like Elvis, to have left the building, while the start-up community, social enterprise, and tech and creative economies are thriving because of nonhierarchical new models. It's no surprise that millennials are ditching post-grad jobs to found start-ups, or that, according to UK headlines, in 2017 "there are now 311,550 company directors under the age of 30, up from 295,890 just two years ago" gracing Britain's economy.[3] These are UK statistics, but show a significant trend that is playing out internationally. Rather than hang around for years waiting to inherit power, a new generation is heading out to take it and make it for themselves.

But it's not just business leadership that's failing to meet the next generation's appetite for a fairer approach to power. In 2016, both the UK and the US saw a surge of youth excite-ment for two left-wing outliers advocating policy that many thought to be consigned to the history books. Septuagenarian socialist Bernie Sanders and sixty-nine-year-old Labour Party leader Jeremy Corbyn's unlikely youth appeal can be captured in the metaphor of their creative hashtags #FeelTheBern and #Grime4Corbyn. There was unprecedented support for this pair of elderly white male politicians among the younger gener-ations principally because both seemed (a) honest and (b) to give a shit. More than any great political statement, this shows (a) what the next generation values and (b) the vacuum of credible alternatives. Individual businesses and politicians can succeed despite an apparent lack of innovation and entrepreneurialism, but it is the absence of optimism and empathy in the system as a whole that might cause fatal damage to the broader structures of conventional mainstream society in the hearts and minds of the coming generation, who expect compassion.

Finally, there is a shift taking place from blind capitalism to woke consumerism. The Aspirationals report is the result of a partnership between New York–based consultancy BBMG and global research company GlobeScan. From representative research in over twenty countries, the report categorizes an emerging mind-set they named the "Aspirationals," who are defined by not just a desire for but also an absolute expectation for "Abundance Without Waste."[4]

They want the same products and services we've all grown up with, they want quality and convenience and cool stuff, but they also have laudably high expectations for how it's produced, where it's from, and what the impact of its journey into their lives is. Action on corruption and environmental damage and fair treatment of staff are all at the top of the Aspirationals' expectations of the brands they'll buy from. And this is not a radical or alternative group. This is me and you. They want the new trainers, the latest tech, and to be able to go out and enjoy themselves. They just don't expect to do it at anyone else's expense. It's not a mind-set defined by age, nor is it grouped to any particular geography or ethnography. It's completely global and across the two reports, three years apart, it's a group who are growing.

The Aspirationals are a "billion-dollar paradigm shift," where the power has been returned to the customer. The report cites Tom LaForge, global director, human & cultural insights, at the Coca-Cola Company: "The harder we compete, the less differentiated we become. As brands sell on functional benefits (what the product is and does for me) and emotional benefits (how I want to feel in this occasion), category after category is being filled with nearly similar products. Large established brands are losing loyalty and market share to newer smaller brands that offer social and cultural benefits."

Raphael Bemporad, founding partner of BBMG, who conceived of and oversaw both studies, neatly sums up the international Aspirational mind-set: "With Aspirationals, the sustainability proposition has changed from being the 'right thing to do' to being the 'cool thing to do.'"

The establishment's thinly veiled self-absorption holds no appeal to these open-minded minds of the future, who want answers, ideas, self-determination, and self-actualization. And herein lies the clue: self-actualization, the famous pinnacle of Maslow's hierarchy of needs, the focus of a thousand leadership books, essays, and TEDx Talks, and a recently reproven mainstay in our understanding of why we do what we do and what we'll do next.

Back in 1943, Abraham Maslow charted a human being's progress through life via a series of "need" states that we attempt to work our way through. Like all good ideas that explain everything, his model is drawn as a triangle.

Pretty much ever since this idea was formulated, we have accepted the notion that we think about morality and the common good only once we've conquered the rungs of property, prosperity, and security. The idea is we begin to give back or meditate on our higher purpose only once we've made it to the top of the pyramid.

But that's the old paradigm. In the new paradigm, there are people whose mind-set is to ponder the value, purpose, and meaning of just about everything from life to work and the balance in between, and as a result they are self-actualizing long before they've climbed that elitist pyramid. Many don't arrive at a point of "giving back" because they never "took" in the first place.

In light of this, I've given Maslow's model an OS update to bring it into the twenty-first century. There are two essential upgrades. First off, I've included Wi-Fi and battery life at the base of the pyramid along with food, shelter, and warmth, because, like, duh.

Second, I've tipped the top of the triangle—the bit when we have our aha moment and realize there's more to life than accumulating stuff—inward and downward. It is my profound observation and belief that for a new generation, self-actualization actually begins at the beginning.

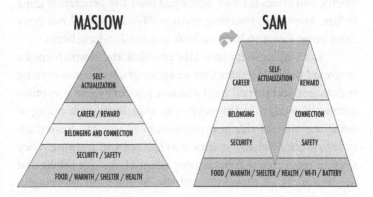

Over the last two decades, I've worked with thousands of young leaders from different countries and cultures who collectively represent the future of leadership. Whether they are urban or rural, middle class or marginalized, their desire to do something meaningful is extremely strong and kicks in early. The much-quoted Millennials Survey produced by global consultancy firm Deloitte supports my Maslow hack: Barry Salzberg, CEO of Deloitte, states: "Millennials are just as interested in how a business develops its people and its contribution to society as they are in its products and profits. This should be an alarm to business, in the way they engage millennial talent or risk being left behind."[5]

Rather than feel pessimistic about current power structures who have vested interests and will protect themselves unto their dying breaths, which in some instances might be better occurring sooner rather than later, I look forward to the next wave of leaders whose understanding of purpose, responsibility, and ethics is more developed than any generation gone before. For them, meaning matters. "Giving a shit" has gone from being a nice-to-have outlook to a need-to-have belief.

In a similar shift toward the practical, the pirates turned a profound belief in values into weapons-grade decision-making techniques and turned hard-and-fast principles into a ruthless competitive edge. In the same way, organizations wanting to make the most of this new mind-set need to move from platitude to attitude when it comes to a clear sense of purpose. They need to recognize that breakaway talent of this age thinks that the best work of their lives will also be the most meaningful work of their lives.

The younger generations coming into the workforce now are naturally more pirate than their predecessors. In order to make sure the new importance they place on meaning and purpose is heard and acted upon, we need to establish new structures that will allow for more collaboration and fairer distribution of power and profit; we need to evolve from the generic twentieth-century business model that was in some ways always built on a degree of exploitation of either their own supply chains and human capital or someone else's creativity or natural resources.

Social Enterprise: Undercover Pirates

Of course, there are already organizations run using an enlightened approach that is both innovative and impact orientated, and they're called social enterprises. If you're unfamiliar with the concept, the term might sound a little bit do-goody, a little bit less serious than nonsocial enterprises, but that impression would be mistaken. I would argue that social entrepreneurs are modern pirates in all but name. A social enterprise is essentially the combination of a very typical business or enterprise model (one that makes money) and a social objective (one that makes a difference). While social enterprises are often income-generating organizations, they don't exist solely to generate profit for shareholders; they share profit and power more fairly than most companies, which in turn makes them more innovative and effective. Overall there is a pirate-like dedication to independence, providing alternative systems and fairness and generating income in a way that's not reliant on the state. (Apart from the plunder, to my mind they're cut from the same cloth.)

The social enterprise name has been around since the 1980s, when it arose as a rebellion against the "greed is good" era of capitalism, but it's begun to tip into mainstream business in a big way. Social enterprise now accounts for approximately 7 percent of all businesses around the world, and as the UK State of Social Enterprise Report 2017 confirms, the sector is out-innovating, out-investing, and out-performing its purely commercial equivalents, with higher rates of diversity, pay equality, and performance, and of course, all while creating positive impact. In short, social enterprise is a thriving international hybrid industry, filling the gulf between big bad business still hooked on growth, inefficient NGOs fundraising themselves into existence, and government policy that can't see past its next election.

There's no wonder social enterprise is doing well, because it taps into (and helps to drive) the shift in values we've been looking at, where doing something that means something is all-important. As the entrepreneur, author, and prolific force of positivity Afdhel Aziz likes to say: *Good Is the New Cool*—the title of his book in which he makes a watertight case for it. It's a neat summary of the coming zeitgeist; partly entrepreneurial, partly socially conscious, and partly about self-actualization. And whereas a combination of those three attributes might have made someone in the past partly worthy, partly wishy-washy, and partly exhausting to hang out with, these really are characteristics that have joined the classic aspiration set that people want to adopt when they grow up, as Afdhel himself demonstrates in both his timely title and as a high-profile, jet-setting public speaker and purpose-driven entrepreneur.

In 2001, when I cofounded Livity, now an international and multiple-award-winning social enterprise and youth-led creative network, I thought I was some sort of pirate-pioneer inventing a new type of business that would make both a difference and some money; I was simultaneously embarrassed and elated when I realized I was in fact just arriving late to the party of a global movement that was already in full swing.

Livity began as an experiment to discover whether "ethical marketing" was an oxymoron, and whether it was possible to bring the budget and influence of brands to create advertising campaigns that would tackle issues that mattered to their audience while still delivering on commercial objectives in a happy sustainable marriage of mutual benefit. Our ambition was to redistribute power and transfer authority away from the big brands who usually like to do the selling to their young audiences who normally like to do the buying. Or to put it another way, we set out to discover whether you could reeducate brand managers to grow their business by seeing young audiences as their responsibility as well as their opportunity.

At the time, the power dynamic between young people and brands was a one-way street. I had spent the last six years running nightclubs, raves, and events and setting up a creative agency and platform called DON'T PANIC from my bedroom. As the music we loved went mainstream, big brands wanted a piece of the action, and as I began working with them, I discovered something that surprised me. Huge numbers of extremely smart and emotionally intelligent people were working overtime with every ounce of creativity they had, spending huge amounts of money desperately trying to create a connection between young people and chewing gum, hair gel, and all the other pointless stuff that no one really needs. At the time I was devastated; I'd finally arrived, but no one with any power was remotely interested in using it usefully. The problem seemed clear and inescapable, so I decided to launch my own rebellion in the form of Livity.

I wanted to take back the power on behalf of the victims of irresponsible marketing. When a brand's core value is "happiness" or "winning" and it directly targets a young, vulnerable, and low-income audience with messages that are deeply sophisticated and powerful at saying, "If you want to be happy or a winner, buy this shit you don't really need for more than you can really afford," young people are in danger of confusing materialism with meaning. This might not be as damaging for the brand's main audience, who are generally affluent and well educated and quite possibly more able to see through the charade, but it can have a profound impact on young people from turbulent, less educated backgrounds with less money and less experience, who confuse the belonging you can buy with the sense of belonging they need, and as a result make a neurological link between important emotions and unimportant promotions.

At the other end of the spectrum, well-meaning charities and government agencies occasionally tried to talk to the same young people about things like sexual or mental health, careers, or keeping out of gangs, but it was often patronizing and out of touch and served only to make the commercial messages appear to be the more compelling solution to their problems.

And so it hit me: the empowering and informative messages most likely to effect a positive life outcome (like avoiding debt or improving diet) are communicated so poorly they make matters worse, while the things that they need the least (like fizzy drinks and $500 sneakers) are communicated so effectively they fill a missing part of who they are as human beings. From that day forward I realized that people in the business of marketing, media, advertising, PR, or communications could choose to be either part of the solution or part of the problem, and that there was little middle ground.

At the time, this was not a conversation brands were having. Enron was still a pinup of corporate social responsibility, and while it was the year Naomi Klein's book *No Logo: Taking Aim at the Brand Bullies* was published, it was still seen as anti-brand, and my idea for Livity was definitely pro-brand AND pro-society. I decided to draw up a list of the smartest people in London's marketing industry, people who might get it and have a good idea of how to right this wrong. I met Michelle, who is now my business partner and who, with more of a formal agency background, had arrived at pretty much the same conclusion as I had. We immediately organized ourselves as quartermaster and captain, equal partners, equally rebellious and equally pirate in nature. We raised the flag of Livity and put the word out that we were beginning a mutiny.

At launch, Michelle and I scraped together the money we could, around £10,000, and we calculated that it would buy us three months of a basic wage, office rent, phone lines, and an internet connection for email (you didn't even need a website in those days). Our rationale was that if we couldn't sell the vision of our marketing rebellion in three months and win a client, then there probably wasn't any value in the idea of an ethical marketing agency after all. Years later I learned this is actually a widely used management strategy called a "burning bridge," whereby you set an inescapable end date to your endeavor to create a sense of urgency and prevent yourself from endlessly chasing the dream. Thankfully, in the last week of our third month, we closed a deal that would see us through our first year.

Two things came to define Livity. The first was a relentless focus on creating only marketing campaigns that delivered on shifting the power between the brand and the audience benefit. The second was the decision that members of that same young audience would be given the keys to the business. Literally.

From Monday to Friday, from dawn to dusk, young people from all backgrounds, walks of life, classes, cultures, and degrees of chaos were able to access the Livity office as if it was their own, and pretty soon it was. They came to work on our in-house publication, *Live* magazine, which was produced entirely by young people, entirely for young people.

Live was protected from the commercial pressure facing the rest of Livity, and the young people were given autonomy and editorial freedom, as well as expert professional mentoring to protect them. From interviews with crack dealers to uncovering the next ten years of underground artists, to an ever popular (with older people) slang dictionary to investigations into all the taboo topics of youth from sexuality to religion, gangs, racism, and policing, it was honest, entertaining, inspiring, authentic, and a center of gravity that brought thousands of young people through our doors, and in turn helped them launch their careers.

In return, it meant our ideas for our clients were the most insight driven, strategically rooted, honest, and effective campaigns they could be. Those young people used the Livity office to start up businesses, begin their careers, do their homework, rehearse plays, write books, and much, much more. Livity provided more than just space for them, but leading-edge technology, desks, computers, studio facilities, mentors, workshops, career advice, and even social work support around housing, benefits, and more. Many young people ended up using Livity as a launch pad for life, allowing them to escape the systemic lack of opportunity they had so far experienced.

Into this noisy, high-energy, chaotic, and creative environment we invited our clients, who became infected with the passion, idealism, and energy as a return on investment. Livity's clients include PlayStation, Google, Netflix, Facebook, Unilever, Barclays bank, and many more. But even more impressive than a roster of iconic logos is the work our young people led for them to develop successful solutions to issues including online bullying, relationship abuse, sexual health awareness, financial literacy, access to employment, future skills, and tackling extremism.

Not all of Livity's initiatives were successful, and we faced some of the hardest obstacles any organization can face, like making redundancies, losing pitches, and worst of all, when challenges would overwhelm one of our young people. But through it all, we held true to our purpose.

We'd built Livity based on passion, for revolution, for change, to make great work, for the creative, impactful, inspiring output, and to empower young people.

And I think this has been the key to Livity's success ever since, across the UK and in South Africa. We defined our values in actions. For many clients, we're the only agency they visit where they aren't the most important people in the room, but take second place to the young people to whom we've so successfully distributed power that they have become indispensable.

Empowering young people to shape, design, lead, and generate great creative work that is both funded and respected by brands they love and also makes a difference to their peers has a transformative effect on everyone involved in the process. We've been called a "transformation engine" by the young people whose lives we've changed, and that idea of a transformer—devolving power, redistributing energy, and accelerating young people's potential—is what defines Livity still, almost twenty years later.

If I sound a little bit proud, that's because I am. I am proud of the hundreds of thousands of young people who have worked with Livity and changed their lives through their own initiative and ideas. Livity gives power to all and champions fairness in every opportunity it pursues. It raises the flag of rebellion, embraces an alternative way of doing business, and magnifies its importance and effect through its collaboration with young people, not through growth. It also creates a safe space where everyone enjoys shared power and fights for fairness, pirate style.

Pirates in a Sea of Waste

There's no shortage of pirate-like social enterprises living out the ideals of redistributing power, making an enemy of exploitation, and fighting for a fairer, more sustainable twenty-first century. A captain among such positive pirates is Kresse Wesling, CEO and founder of Elvis & Kresse.

Wesling says she's always been fascinated by waste, even as a child; going to the dump with her dad she'd see beautiful old things in need of someone to repurpose them where other people simply saw rubbish.

In 2005, Wesling had been thinking about setting up a business in repurposing waste, but she wasn't sure what type of waste she wanted to use or what her end product should be. Then she happened to meet some people from the London Fire Brigade on a course. From them she learned that damaged fire hose is thrown away as waste. Made of thick rubber, fire hose is pretty much the least recyclable thing known to humanity and was adding to the huge problem that is overspilling landfill sites. She realized that waste fire hose was the raw material of her dreams, and that this was a big problem that she was sure she could help solve.

Wesling scraped together some basic funding to get started and convinced the London Fire Brigade that it would be better to give her the decommissioned hose rather than pay to send it to landfill. She promised them that if her idea worked, she'd give them 50 percent of all her profits.

At first Wesling thought the hose might make good roof tiles for sheds. She was wrong. Research revealed that cut hose is no longer fireproof, and after ten years it would crack. Leaky flammable roofing was not a winner. But then she turned her eye to sustainable fashion and settled on bags. When she started to look for someone who could help her transform the waste hose, she realized the craftspeople with the necessary skills to work on such a tough material were spread widely, mostly in mainland Europe, and were not keen to work with what she had to offer. After a lengthy search, a partner with the requisite top-end craftsmanship pedigree was found. She finally persuaded this manufacturer to work with her, and together they produced a collection of beautiful handbags and wallets that combined ethics and aesthetics, waste and luxury. One of her early wins was persuading Apple to let her make a reclaimed fire hose iPhone case, which was stocked exclusively in their flagship London Apple Store. When a stylist picked one of her belts to use in a photo shoot with Cameron Diaz that ended up on the cover of *Vogue*, Elvis & Kresse found a new meaning of power for their products.

Once she had been recognized by one of the most powerful platforms in the hard-to-infiltrate world of high fashion, Wesling knew how to use that power and built her own brand while diversifying into new and more difficult waste products. Now Elvis & Kresse reclaim ten different forms of waste, including the sacking that coffee beans and tea leaves are shipped in, offset printers' blankets, and parachute silk.

The company is run as a social enterprise, meaning it's entirely independent, it generates its own trading income, and it uses its profits partly to fund growth and partly to donate to social and environmental causes. It was founded on the dual basis of fixing a problem, in this case an environmental one, and developing a product that would make a profit. The promised 50 percent of profit on the fire hose was and continues to be duly transferred to the Fire Fighters Charity. That original pledge has mutated into one of three measures the company uses to evaluate success: not just the financial bottom line but also how many tons of waste are diverted from landfill and how much money is donated to charity. It is a transparent organization, welcoming visitors to its offices and workshops. Elvis & Kresse has shifted the manufacturing skills it needs back to the UK by training apprentices, so more of its lines can be produced domestically, and the operation is run entirely on renewable energy.

Wesling has so much restless energy and radical intention that she could teach most pirates a lesson. She generates ideas at top speed and relentlessly hunts down solutions. She's totally unsentimental about wanting to do good, and she makes doing good look incredibly stylish. She attributes her success to her small team of people who are as invested as she is in honoring the raw materials, the process, and the customer.

And the moment Wesling knew that Elvis & Kresse was a success was not when her product made the cover of *Vogue*, or because of the numerous social enterprise awards and the recognition she received from celebrity clients and No. 10 Downing Street. Instead, it was when she realized that she'd basically made herself (or more accurately, her handbags) redundant. By 2010 the business was sustainably using all the country's waste hoses; as long as it keeps doing so, the hose problem is solved. Some people might feel a little anxious if the source material of their most iconic product was thus limited, but not Wesling. She's now working with firefighters around the world, taking delivery of their waste hose, and at the same time she's on to the next thing: taking on the colossal waste problem in the luxury leather industry. At the end of 2017 she announced that she was going into partnership with Burberry Foundation to reclaim 120 tons of Burberry leather scraps over the next five years and turn them into new products. She's found a new, even bigger puzzle to solve.

Wesling's story epitomizes the idea that if power is redistributed publicly and accountably, the purity of a strong idea can be protected and accelerated as it compounds, growing its impact as it does. Wesling deftly devolves power to a wider group of suppliers, stakeholders, and customers, making them all complicit in achieving the goal while also making them all protectors of the vision.

Just like our Golden Age pirate predecessors, we find ourselves in uncertain and unfair times but with a fundamental desire to do things differently. We've seen that even with the energy of rebellion, a keen crew, and cutting-edge reorganizational skills, until there's a shift in power dynamics away from hierarchies and toward collective and representative models, our ability to change things is limited. Like the Golden Age pirates, we need new values, clearly articulated, to replace the old ones that worship financial profit above all.

When you commit to redistributing power and fighting for fairness, you take the single most radical and effective step toward making your change a long-lasting success. When you give power away, it will flourish and multiply. Other people will be inspired by your actions and will start to follow suit. Inspired by innovation, the mainstream will begin to adopt the behavior of pirates, like social enterprises who start out at the edge. It was pirates' collective effort and focus on both financial and social justice that allowed them to thrive and take on the world.

Their sense of mission or "purpose," their crusade against unfairness, and their ability to influence change, whether implicit or explicit, were fundamental components of the pirates' success—their legacy and their impact. It was their clarion call, and it was heard the world over.

If we've learned anything about pirates, it's that their practices are often an accurate prediction of how waves coming from the edges of society will influence the mainstream. I would bet all my pieces of eight that the tactics and techniques of transferring power that are making the modern pirates of the social enterprise movement so successful and so attractive to work for are a rising wave that will become mainstream practice within my lifetime.

In fact, pretty soon, I suspect, any organization operating by any other standards will begin to be perceived as a distinctly antisocial enterprise.

There's never a man looked me between the eyes and seen a good day afterward.

—Long John Silver

We've covered a lot in this chapter, so we're going to keep the reflection simple. If you can avoid the urge to skip it, it's often held up as one of the most valuable exercises in all the Be More Pirate workshops we've run.

The question is, When it comes to power, how will you be more pirate? How will you share it out? How will you protect it and how will you protect yourself from it? What principles do you respect so much you'd take a risk for them? What values do you treasure so much that you'd be willing to suffer to protect them? And what ideals do you hold so dear that you'd be willing to lose something you love to defend them?

You can use the space provided to note down your answer to this question:

What principles, values, or ideals are you willing to fight for?

When I say fight, I mean actually fight. That doesn't have to be physical; it could be a fight with the system, a professional conflict, a falling-out with a friend, or a row with a stranger. It could be a war of words, it could be a battle of wills, or it could be lobbying, arguing, demonstrating, or debating.

But whatever it is, it's a real fight, one where you're putting your neck on the line, you could get hurt, you've got something to lose. It could cost you your job, end a relationship, damage your reputation, or worse.

This one isn't easy; if you get to five, you'll have more than most people.

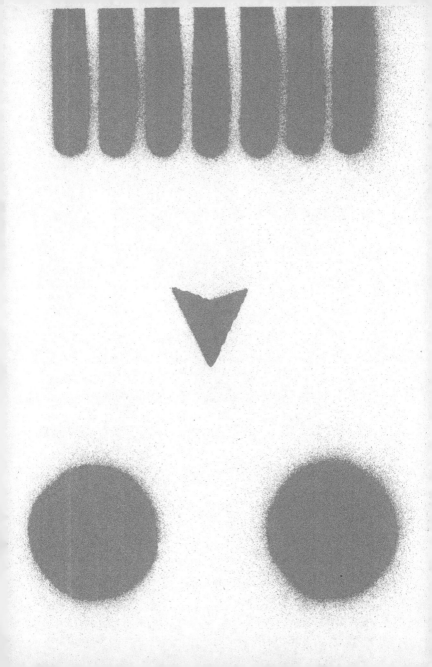

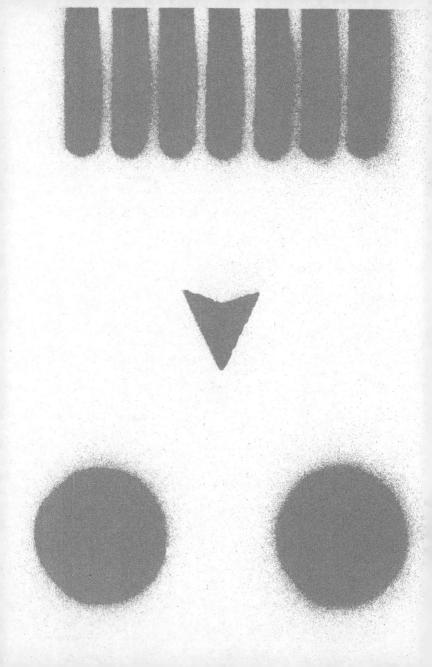

8. RETELL TALL TALES

Or How to Weaponize Stories and Tell the Hell Out of Them

Dead Men Tell No Tales

Welcome to the fifth of five rounds, and now for the knockout. From the last four steps you have an idea of how you can rebel against the status quo, rewrite the rules to make them better, reorganize yourself to achieve scale rather than pointless growth, and redistribute power to protect your principles. But what's next? What's the final step to being more pirate? It's about how you tell your story so the world listens. In this chapter we're going to discover how pirates used spectacular storytelling techniques that made the whole world pay attention.

Pirates didn't just tell stories, they creatively weaponized the art of storytelling. When they unfurled the pirate flag, the black background embellished with bones, skulls, skeletons, bleeding hearts, and all manner of visual metaphors, they were taking the ultimate symbol of the establishment, the flag (also the principal method of all maritime communications), and desecrating it so that it screamed rebellion and created a global icon. Pirates cultivated and curated their own myth, ably abetted by a new mass media hungry for great stories. They told fierce tales about themselves so that others would tell them again and again. Their stories wove into the fabric of culture and ordinary people's imaginations with storytelling serving to pull together the last four steps of change. The pirates' ideals infiltrated society and culture to influence the mainstream.

The pirates achieved a far-reaching legacy, and though you might not aspire to achieve their level of mythical status, there is a lot to be learned from the way pirates wrote their way into culture because today it's vital to tell your story right if you want to get the attention you deserve and the audience you desire. Being able to communicate your idea effectively is often as important as coming up with the idea itself. And though you might think it's better to test your idea or its message by placing it somewhere comfortable, somewhere you know your message will be well received, a pirate might recommend you do the opposite. The usual approach is to start somewhere friendly, with a receptive audience, by contacting someone you know will be sympathetic to your mission—maybe via the social media feed of a friend, or maybe you'd even pay a little to place your message in front of people you know will like it.

The *unusual* method, and the one I'm recommending you try, is to go the other way, the pirate way, and take your storytelling to the most dangerous, contentious, or incendiary place possible, in order to magnify those stories' effect. The strategy and creative directors at Livity, Katy Woodrow Hill and James Hogwood, came up with this method and called it the Lion's Den.

The Lion's Den approach encourages you to go somewhere unexpected, somewhere that scares you, where you might be likely to offend, where you risk being rejected but where you will inadvertently strengthen your story because the reaction of others will amplify it or their very criticisms will force you to tell it better next time. It's a bold approach, but it's effectively what the pirates did: sailed their antiestablishment symbol right into the establishment's view and used the repercussions to create the world's first global superbrand.

Coca-Cola is usually considered the world's first superbrand, established through its memorable logo and signature bottle design in the late 1800s, but over a hundred years before, the pirates got there first. Pirates built a killer brand through their ability to tell a tall tale and raise a fearsome flag. They instinctively knew that a real brand is built on more than a clever logo or a cool name. A powerful brand is an emotional tool that demands the mental availability of its audience to signal a clear message. In their case, the pirate flag said "surrender or die."

Scary as that sounds, the pirates pioneered reputation management so they could actually be less violent and command the high seas through fear, not fighting. Each captain and crew had a different flag, or Jolly Roger, flying from their mast, but there were common elements found across all pirate flags: a black background, bleeding hearts, knives and daggers, skulls, skeletons (sometimes dancing ones), bones, and hourglasses coming together to threaten death, murder, and mayhem. Calico Jack Rackham (Anne Bonny's boyfriend, if you remember him) is responsible for designing the specific flag that is now taken as the definitive emblem of piracy, the skull above crossed bones. The well-timed and dramatic display of the pirate flag was intended to strike paralyzing fear into any target and was sometimes followed by the startling appearance of the entire pirate crew on deck, resplendent in face paints, with smoking homemade grenades, actual rattling of sabers, and blood-curdling screams.

These theatrics weren't employed just because pirates loved melodrama and dressing up (well, maybe just a bit); they were used to send a clear message to anyone who came in their path: "There is nowhere to hide, we're coming for everything you've got. Surrender or die." This is branding, this is story-telling, and this is how it's done, pirate style.

And the really clever bit about it is that they were not just communicating a message. They were also advancing a strategic goal. You see, the pirate's "killer" branding was first and foremost a technique that protected their valuable reputa-tion, which in turn drove their profitability. Remember, pirates had no incentive for real violence other than in small doses to reinforce their brand. Ammunition and recruits were expensive to replace. Stopping for repairs was extremely risky. Pirates really didn't want to damage a vessel they intended to steal, or one they might need to escape in. Pirates also had that unique and expensive policy of compensating their injured with financial payouts, so they didn't want anyone getting seriously hurt, since that would eat into their collective earnings. All in all, both strategically and tactically, it was far more sensible for pirates to avoid costly conflicts and put all their piratical story-telling efforts into creating panic on sight to achieve a low-cost, high-return surrender scenario. Admittedly, the reputation be-hind a brand has to be protected, and so pirates had to "live the brand" from time to time. But aside from the aforementioned 5 percent or so of psychopaths in their ranks, the terror they are so famous for was in truth used sparingly and strategically for brand building and, ultimately, to minimize their recourse to violence.

The Baddest Beard of All

There can be no greater example of an individual pirate for whom this general observation rings true than the infamous Edward Teach, better known as Blackbeard. Of course all of us have heard of him, the most badass beard in piratical history, the greatest seafaring strategist, the most revered leader, the lustiest old swashbuckler with fifteen or so "wives" to his name, and the most villainous and salty sea dog. At least that's what we think we know. But you could sail a galleon through the gap between what we think we know about Blackbeard and the actual truth.

Blackbeard wasn't the most successful pirate of the Golden Age (that would be Black Bart), nor the richest (that would have been Sam Bellamy), nor did he score the greatest haul ever (Henry Avery) or have the longest career (Henry Morgan). In fact his career lasted about two years and his most famous raid (the blockade of what is now Charleston, in South Carolina) ended up seizing a box of medicines. But when it came to telling tall tales, Blackbeard didn't just punch above his weight—he became the reputational equivalent of a knockout in the first round. Blackbeard's reputation as lover, fighter, rascal, and rogue was, of course, helped by the fact he had a massive ship. Commanding a stolen slave boat he pimped up for pirating, loaded with cannons and renamed *Queen Anne's Revenge*, in two short years of infamy he took the pirate "brand" to the next level and became a household name.

As Angus Konstam states in his biography of Blackbeard:

Almost single-handedly he engineered the pirate crisis that swept North America in the summer of 1718. . . . The panic Blackbeard created was out of all proportion to the number of ships he seized or the goods he plundered. Blackbeard's notoriety—the reason he couldn't be allowed to live—was achieved at the expense of the confidence of an emerging nation. That is what made him such a fearsome figure, and why his image, if not his exploits, is still remembered today.[1]

Blackbeard had some trademark techniques that contributed to this most fearsome reputation. (I'll let you assess which you might be able to use in your next meeting.) He took the pirate flag and, like many captains, made it his own. His version showed a skeleton toasting a glass to Satan in one hand and skewering a bleeding heart with the other, adding a macabre devil-may-care air to a symbol that already meant death.

Blackbeard's Three Rules of Branding

Rule 1: Find the singular message and make it unignorable.

One of Blackbeard's signature fear-inducing techniques was to set light to sulfurous fuses at the plaited ends of his long and famous beard to create a smoldering, fizzing, crackling, and pantaloon-staining vision of fear. It was designed to help him appear to live up to the reputation he himself cultivated, that he was indeed from hell. This,

added to an all-black getup, a brace of pistols across his
chest, and cutlasses at both sides, ensured his reality lived
up to his stories and froze his enemies in fear. In his 1724 account of all things piratical, Captain Charles Johnson, the
coauthor of *A General History of the Pyrates*, wrote:

*Captain Teach assumed the cognomen of Blackbeard, from that
large quantity of hair, which, like a frightful meteor, covered his
whole face, and frightened America more than any comet that
has appeared there in a long time. This beard was black, which
he suffered to grow of an extravagant length; as to breadth, it
came up to his eyes; he was accustomed to twist it with ribbons,
in small tails . . . and turn them about his ears: in time of
action, he wore a sling over his shoulders, with three brace
of pistols, hanging in holsters like bandoliers; and stick lighted
matches under his hat, which appearing on each side of his face,
his eyes naturally looking fierce and wild, made him altogether
such a figure, that imagination cannot form an idea of a fury,
from Hell, to look more frightful.*[2]

Blackbeard clearly took fancy dress, I mean branding, to a
whole other level. He would cast such terror into the
hearts of his victims that those who lived (which was most
of them because, ironically enough, either despite his fero-
cious reputation or because of it, some historians argue
there are no verified accounts of him actually killing anyone) would be sure to tell the tale . . . which was of course
the whole point. It's not enough just to tell tales, you have
to tell *tall* tales. Tell stories that make people shit the bed,

not just bedtime stories. Build legends, build myths, build a legacy.

Rule 2: Don't just live the brand, be the brand.

While he may have avoided unnecessary death, Blackbeard is said to have indulged in the odd show of violence, all in the name of brand maintenance. Philip Gosse said in *The Pirate Who's Who* that "there was that little affair in the cabin, when Teach blew out the candle and in the dark fired his pistols under the table for no other reason, than 'if he did not shoot one or two of them now and then, they'd forget who he was.'"[3]

Rule 3: Protect your reputation; give people something to gossip about.

Blackbeard told stories to aid his strategy. He was all about the profit, all about the plunder, all about the pieces of eight. The image he created for himself and the pirate way of life stopped people in their tracks and prevented them from challenging him. So successful was Blackbeard's storytelling that his reputation far exceeded his deeds. With the help of the establishment, the hungry and salacious media presented Blackbeard as a murderous villain, but in reality Blackbeard never killed a soul while a pirate. Colin Woodard explains: "In the dozens of eyewitness accounts of his victims, there is not a single instance in which he killed anyone prior to his final, fatal battle with the Royal

Navy."[4] Some might go so far as to say that this was Blackbeard's single biggest achievement: that the most feared pirate of the Golden Age never actually killed anybody is a testament to his storytelling power.

Well-Told Stories

The pirates told thermonuclear stories that made superior and stronger opponents take note and in some instances allowed them to avoid a fight altogether. Their stories infiltrated society and their ideas were woven into common culture. But how does a simple, well-told story compound interest, gather momentum, and go on to change the world? How do the radical and experimental ideas aboard the chaos of a pirate ship have any connection to the civilization we enjoy today? Back in Chapter 2 we explored the crucial role that piracy plays in driving innovation. Remember the pirates' approach to injury compensation which developed into social insurance, pirate radio that led to the BBC opening up more channels, and online music piracy that led to iTunes? Well, it turns out the pirates weren't just influencing the mainstream because they were shouting about their ideas and weaponizing storytelling. They were directly influencing the mainstream because some of them were actually in cahoots with the established powers of the day, telling them their stories face-to-face. In his book *The Pirates' Pact*, author, academic, and historian Douglas Burgess Jr. put forward a meticulously researched argument that even though the British governors of the American colonies were officially at war with

the "enemies of humanity," in reality it seems there was exten-
sive collusion between them.[5] When Blackbeard was killed in
combat, numerous letters were recovered from his cabin, and
many of them carried the seal of the royal governor of His
Majesty's Colony North of Carolina, Governor Eden. This
correspondence indicates that deals were being done between
the king's officers and at least one of the world's most notorious pirates on an ongoing basis. Blackbeard was public enemy
number one, yet there he was having regular correspondence
with a state governor (who would soon form a coup against the
king). Philip Gosse in *The Pirate Who's Who* even cites evidence
that puts the same Governor Eden as a guest of honor at one
of Blackbeard's many weddings.[6] The two sides thought to be
in opposition weren't just providing protections to each other,
they weren't just doing a few under-the-counter deals, they
were forming deep, meaningful relationships with each other.
And as their stories would evolve, so would their significance;
the role the pirates played on behalf of the colonial governors
was one of undermining the security of tax and trade income
for the British government, which helped to establish economic
independence away from the control of a faraway king. You see,
in a way, the colonial governors of America wanted the same
freedoms the pirates had snatched for themselves and, in a far
more covert fashion, were adopting some of the techniques
they'd learned from the pirates' tall tales.

It was the entirely fictional pirate Captain Jack Sparrow
who said, "You can always trust the untrustworthy because
you can always trust that they will be untrustworthy. It's the
trustworthy you can't trust," which feels ironically adept for

summarizing the revelation that in some small way the story of pirate independence is a precursor to American independence.

During the Golden Age there were secret relationships forming between established enemies that cast a shadow over who was on whose side and who was on the "good" side. In a tale-telling double bluff, both parties continued to let the public lap up the widely publicized story that bloodthirsty pirates were outmaneuvering His Majesty's Royal Navy and plundering Spanish gold. But behind the curtain, there were players writing an alternative script on both sides. Some governors provided protection from the law, a blind eye here and there along with the odd royal pardon, and in return the pirates provided them with an income from the gold they stole and protection when they needed it. Pirate ideas found their way onto the desks of power and were written into history because they were in cahoots with the men in charge who were officially their enemy. While the British at home had, in Burgess's words, "failed to reckon with the powerful lure of the colonial anti model; piracy not as a crime, but as a legitimate occupation; pirates not as 'enemies of the human race' but as respected members of the community acting with the cognizance and collaboration of powerful gubernatorial patrons," the American governors under British rule were more open to it.[7]

After more than a hundred years of colonial rule in America, rebellion was in the air. Governors were starting to express their frustration, and war with the British and the consequent independence of the United States was just decades away. These governors, some of whom would go on to be the founding fathers of the United States, needed the help of insurgents who held no allegiance to the crown and could keep a secret—they needed nothing less than a militia. Now, where to find a well-armed militia for hire that could secretly engage in early and underhanded maneuvers to frustrate the British . . .

The future founding fathers, some of whom had investments in the plantations of the Caribbean and had set their sights on achieving power, had taken note of the success that the pirates' alternative community had gained, both financially and socially. They had witnessed the proto-democratic pirate republic bubbling up under their noses in Nassau, and they had learned its lessons. They understood why it had gained such popular support and won the hearts and imaginations of ordinary working people, but they also saw why and where it failed.

They harnessed the power and potency of the pirates' techniques and well-told stories to establish the defining moment in American history in the eighteenth century, that of boxing Britain into an ever-tighter corner in an explosion that would usher in a new age of independence.

Now, it would be naive to draw too direct a line between the pirates' inspirational tactics and American independence, but it would be equally naive to imagine the governors' interactions with pirates did not have some effect and influence.

In the absolutely brilliant Pirate History Podcast, its host and historian Matt Albers explains his strongly held view about the lineage from pirates to founding fathers, from the role they contributed to subverting taxes and to economic independence from England through to the growing weight of the threat they represented of a new order. Albers provides an eloquent indication of how strong the pirate story of rebellion became, and how far its reach was felt:

> The tree of American republican democracy is rooted in West Indian piracy. The Caribbean pirates of the seventeenth and eighteenth centuries practiced the crudest and purest form of democratic self-rule that gave each crew member a vote and a voice, regardless of race, religion, gender, or sexuality. Those outlaws who had been cast out from the polite society of old Europe were forced to see the world through pluralistic, democratic eyes, and that view erupted in a century of revolutionary violence that would shake the foundations of empires and culminate in the Age of Revolution.[8]

The ever-effacing Albers pays all credit to his sources, but his analysis of the material is both entertaining and enlightening, and on this topic he pointed me toward the aforementioned Douglas Burgess for further evidence.

Burgess makes an in-depth assessment of the alliances between pirates and the colonial governors, some of whom would become the founding fathers, in a way that suggests the influence between the two was undeniable, even if it took another fifty years or so to transpire into anything as specific as the Declaration of Independence:

> Piracy—forever maligned, obscured, or misinterpreted as the pirates' rebellion against the status quo—was indeed a radical challenge to the English state. Yet that challenge

came not from the pirates themselves. It was their patrons, the earnest colonial governors, who through quiet accord and longstanding practice signaled the limits of crown law and the germination of a distinct Atlantic community. A community that would one day be known as the United States of America.[9]

There's no doubt that the pirates' innovations and forward-thinking attitudes influenced mainstream society. The Golden Age pirates were master storytellers and they established their legacy by permeating the culture of the day. From pioneering the world's first superbrand via the Jolly Roger to creating their own mythical image via body paint and smoking beards, their tactics captured popular imagination and earned them their place in history. The pirates took their story right into the lion's den when they formed alliances with officials who had the power to have them tried and hanged. As a consequence, not only did they make more money, more efficiently, but also their values and ideas were granted another lease on life on an even bigger stage.

The Remarkable Tale of Daryl Davis

It might not be immediately clear why a blues pianist from the 1980s is a modern pirate, but if you don't know his story, hold on to your tricorn hat for a lesson in weaponized storytelling. However, inspiring though his story may be, please do not try this at home.

Davis has spent years playing the piano alongside musical

legends like Chuck Berry and Jerry Lee Lewis. One night in 1983 he was playing in a "white" bar called the Silver Dollar Lounge when one of the audience came up to him to tell him that he'd never heard a black man play as well as Jerry Lee Lewis. When Davis told the guy that, actually, Lewis had learned to play from listening to black boogie-woogie musicians and was a friend of his, the conversation took a turn. Davis started to get the feeling that his new acquaintance had never really spoken to a black man before. So he asked the man if this was the case, and if it was so, then why? The man replied, "Because I am a member of the Ku Klux Klan," and then showed Davis his membership card to prove it.

Rather than run for the hills, Davis decided to do something not all of us would do but could do with doing more often. He didn't step away, he stepped up. He invited that Klansman to share a beer and swap stories about music and musicians. That night, a deeply unlikely friendship was established. Years later, when the two met again, Davis found himself the first black American to own a Klan cloak, because its owner had handed it over to him in surrender to the power of a well-told tale.

Davis continued to share stories with the Klan, in senior members' homes but also at their events and rallies. These conversations and storytelling sessions were his way of fighting one of the most powerful, well-organized, terrifying, and violently racist groups ever to have existed. And it worked. It worked really well. As Davis said:

You challenge them. But you don't challenge them rudely or violently. You do it politely and intelligently. And when

you do things that way, chances are they will reciprocate
and give you a platform. So he and I would sit down and
listen to one another over a period of time. And the cement that held his ideas together began to get cracks in it.
And then it began to crumble. And then it fell apart.[10]

Davis weaponized storytelling to deweaponize racism in his
backyard. Using his anecdotal approach, he changed perspectives of ingrained prejudice and took the robes of the three
most senior Klan members in Maryland, since when the group
has been unable to reorganize itself back into any sort of power
across the whole state.

You'd think the institutions whose remit it was to tackle
racism would be interested, supportive, and keen to build on
Davis's success, but unfortunately they didn't see eye to eye
with his pirate approach. As Davis tells it:

I had one guy from the local NAACP [National Association for the Advancement of Colored People] branch
chew me up one side and down the other, saying, "You
know, we've worked hard to get ten steps forward. Here
you are sitting down with the enemy having dinner, you're
putting us twenty steps back." I pull out my robes and
hoods and say, "Look, this is what I've done to put a dent
in racism. I've got robes and hoods hanging in my closet
by people who've given up that belief because of *my* conversations sitting down to dinner. They gave it up. How
many robes and hoods have you collected?" And then they
shut up.[11]

The lengths Davis went to were extreme and admirable, but also dangerous—he literally entered the lion's den to tell his story. Hopefully, you won't need to put yourself in harm's way to make waves with your tales, but keep Davis in mind as you think about how to distill your message and tell your story in a way that will evoke an emotional response in your target audience and resonate far further than if you'd just tried to appeal to the most obvious audience. Davis proves that we don't have to tell the loudest story or speak to the biggest audience to achieve great results.

Speak Softly, but Carry a Big Can of Paint

Banksy has used the way he tells stories to change the world. He is a master among modern pirates, changing people's perceptions, mocking the establishment, altering institutions, amassing legions of followers, and opening up new rules for art. Through his signature stencil street graffiti, he has become a world-renowned artist, whose work criticizes practically every institution you can think of, including the art industry itself. The first of his stencil pieces was a picture of a teddy bear hurling a Molotov cocktail at three riot police that appeared in his hometown of Bristol in 1997, and his most recent work can be found on the streets of Palestine. Banksy routinely parodies all forms of the establishment, from the military to the monarchy to the police force, with iconic and emblematic imagery that usually represents society through the invocation of either children, the elderly, monkeys, or rats.

The rats are among the most consistent characters Banksy

uses when it comes to ridiculing the rules. Some observers have suggested Banksy's liberal use of the humble rat is because the word is an anagram of art; others believe it's a representation of Banksy himself, as the animal emerges at night to cause a nuisance. The ever-quotable rebel has his own explanation that speaks more directly to rule breaking. "If you feel dirty, insignificant, or unloved, then rats are a good role model. They exist without permission, they have no respect for the hierarchy of society, and they have sex fifty times a day."

Banksy's work on public walls has included rats as paparazzi, rats announcing the end of the world, rats as businessmen, and rats as rats carrying placards giving advice to humans that ranged from "If graffiti changed anything it would be illegal" to "Let them eat crack." As his work caught the public imagination, it didn't just stimulate interest and awareness in street art, it also planted the idea of creative activism in the public mind-set. He's continually used the platform of his art to provoke debate on important contemporary issues. The greater the taboo, often the greater the challenge: a lynched Ku Klux Klan member in a white hooded suit stenciled on a wall in Birmingham, Alabama, a child in a sweatshop making bunting for the London 2012 Olympics on a wall just outside the arena ahead of the opening ceremony, and even a life-size dummy wearing an immediately recognizable orange Guantánamo Bay jumpsuit with a sack over its head chained to a fence in Disneyland, causing the park to be shut down. I mean, Lion's Den, anyone? In December 2011 he unveiled *Cardinal Sin*, a bust of an eighteenth-century Catholic priest with his face pixelated out using the same technique used to protect the identity of victims of sex offenders. This was before widespread acknowledgment of the church's history of institutionalized pedophilia had been made and public outrage was growing. Banksy's official explanation, as reported by BBC News, only added fuel to the fire: "At this time of year it's easy to forget the true meaning of Christianity—the lies, the corruption, the abuse." To Banksy's credit, every time his popularity or accessibility catches up with him, he takes another step away from the mainstream and opts to push boundaries even further. When the "Banksy effect" led to an explosion of interest in street art, some of his work achieved record figures at Sotheby's auction house. Banksy's response was to release a stencil of a crowded art auction centered around a canvas emblazoned with the words "I can't believe you morons actually buy this shit."

Most recently his work has moved to the infamous West Bank Wall, the contentious 400-mile barrier separating Palestine and Israel. What began with provocative, imaginative, and bitingly funny observations has resulted in a pop-up hotel called the Walled Off Hotel, where you can stay in Banksy-adorned rooms, take stencil-art master classes, and put your own statement on the wall alongside Banksy's masterpieces.

This culminated in late 2017 with an event typifying the classic British street party with cakes, bunting, and Union flags to satirize the anniversary of the Balfour Declaration that first promised a Jewish homeland in Palestine. The centerpiece of the "performance" was the unveiling of a "royal apology" subverting the royal initials into the message: "ER . . . Sorry." Banksy's statement read: "This conflict has brought so much suffering to people on all sides—it didn't feel appropriate to 'celebrate' the

British role . . . The British didn't handle things well here. When you organize a wedding [referring to the promises made by the UK government], it's best to make sure the bride isn't already married."[12]

Banksy has stood up to so many aspects of the status quo, created a following, a platform, and a movement, turned society's gaze onto the powerless, and delivered weapon-strength messages and stories, none more powerful than the one he never told, his identity. Banksy's true identity remains to this day a mystery. When it comes to breaking the rules that others feel obliged to follow, Banksy is a pirate of the highest order. In his own words: "The greatest crimes in the world are not committed by people breaking the rules but by people following the rules." For us pirates, ready to catapult our ideas into the stratosphere, there are many lessons to draw from Banksy's work. First, if emotion is key to good storytelling, so too is humor, intrigue, and irreverence. Try to include and provoke a couple of these sentiments in the stories you tell.

The rest of the lessons are best delivered by the master pirate himself, from his own book of quotations *Banging Your Head Against a Brick Wall*:[13]

- *Art should comfort the disturbed and disturb the comfortable.*

  Know which side you're on and tell your story accordingly to give confidence to and grow your community, and at the same time strike some fear and uncertainty into the heart of your enemy.

- *Think outside the box, collapse the box, and take a fucking sharp knife to it.*

Do all you can to expand your thinking, don't tell the obvious story, and once you've found it, enter the Lion's Den and tell it to the person or group least likely to buy it. Spend as much time thinking it through as you expect to spend shouting it out.

- *A wall is a very big weapon. It's one of the nastiest things you can hit someone with.*

The medium you choose is always part of the message; and many have said the medium *is* the message. Choose it carefully, use it wisely, and your audience will pay as much attention to where and how you share your story as they will do to what you say.

Back when I was running DON'T PANIC, we collaborated with Banksy on a poster that would be distributed for free all over London. We had decided to attack the big oil companies, so Joe Wade (now the CEO of DON'T PANIC) and I wrote the words and Banksy created one of his trademark pieces to go with them. It was a family on a beach holiday about to blow themselves up, as the father was lighting a cigarette right next to an enormous oil spill on the sand. When I explained I was hoping the project would "politicize consumers," Banksy laughed quite hard at my naive optimism. I imagine he'd laugh even harder if he ever sees I've tried to turn his quotes into any sort of lesson, so I'll stop here. We can't all be Banksy.

From rebel to retell, you've gone the full five pirate change-inducing rounds. You are armed to the teeth with techniques that many generations of pirate-like individuals and organizations have been adopting and refining in order to change the world. And so here ends the five pirate stages of change. But before we move into Part Three to discuss the power of the Pirate Code, I invite you to complete the following exercise.

A story is true. A story is untrue. As time extends it matters less and less. The stories we want to believe . . . those are the ones that survive.

—Calico Jack Rackham

We've seen that a well-told story can change the course of history, we've focused on the techniques the pirates mastered, and we've understood the impact.

Now it's time to consider your own legend.

I'd like you to take a few minutes to consider the following question:

Who is the scariest, most difficult, controversial, or provocative audience for your story?

Try to make it to five distinctively different audiences. In the workshops that's around the number we aim for, because it's not an easy challenge, but once a few individual Lion's Dens emerge, suddenly nearly every participant has had that moment when they suddenly see a place to tell their tale that will create more traction, action, and reaction than any advertising spend, PR, or traditional promotion to a friendly audience could achieve.

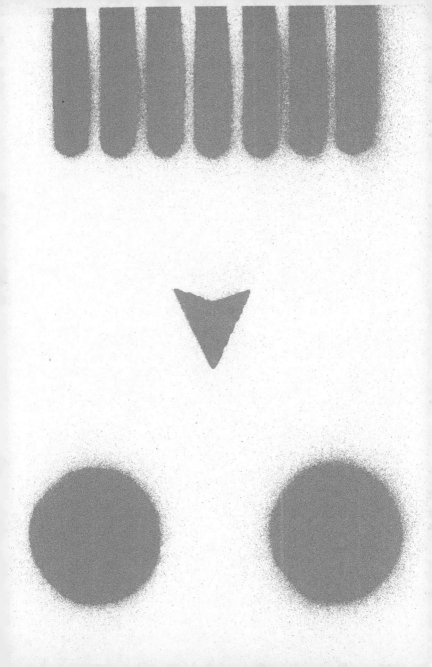

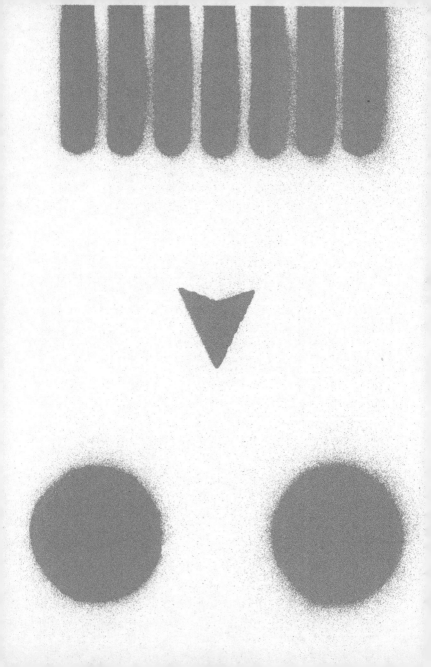

9. BY THE NUMBERS

To make the pirates' history relatable and their influence easy for you to understand, over the last five chapters I've presented their practices and philosophy that led to radical change in a five-part structured framework, and in doing so I've risked turning the pirates' rebellious nature into a formulaic exercise.

But these radicals can't be summarized entirely in managementspeak, nor can their lessons be squeezed into an easily digestible leadership workshop (although I do a great one). To provide a more suitably fluid overview of the pirates' anarchic architecture of influence, here are some key facts and figures from over three hundred years of piracy in all its forms. I'll leave you to join up the dots.

2,000

In 1671, 2,000 men took part in the raid led by Henry Morgan on Panama City, one of the largest pirate fleets ever assembled.

1,000

In 1717, the governor of Bermuda estimated there were 1,000 active pirates by a "modest computation."

13,000

The average strength of the Royal Navy following mass redundancies at the end of the Spanish War of Succession in any given year between 1716 and 1726 was 13,000.

80

The average number of crew members aboard a pirate ship during the Golden Age was 80.

200

Sam Bellamy's crew, one of the larger such bodies in 1717, was made up of 200 "Brisk Men."

28.2

The average age of a pirate during the Golden Age was 28.2 years.

50

The oldest pirate on record during the Golden Age was 50.

14

The youngest pirate on record during the Golden Age was 14.

57

During the Golden Age, 57 percent of pirates were in their twenties.

£25

The average annual salary in the Merchant Navy during the Golden Age was £25 (equal to approximately £10,000 in 2018).

£1,000

The reward from a raid Henry Morgan led in 1695 was £1,000 a man, once evenly distributed (equal to roughly £400,000 in 2018).

25–30

During the Golden Age 25 to 30 percent of pirate crew members were black.

60

In the year of his final defeat and death in 1718, 60 percent of Blackbeard's crew were believed to be black, which is the highest percentage ever recorded for any pirate ship.

400

During his brief career from 1719 to 1722, Black Bart seized over 400 ships, by far the most prizes of any pirate captain.

148

The highest number of pirates hanged in any given year was 148 in 1722.

15 million

When pirate radio launched in the UK in 1964, it was listened to by approximately 15 million people, which was about a third of the population at the time.

4

The BBC launched 4 new radio stations in response to pirate radio by 1967.

600

Some 600 pirate radio stations operated around the UK in 1989, before legislation cracked down in 1990.

67

In 2007, 67 percent of UK citizens said they still believed pirate radio played music you can't get on other stations.

70

In 2011, 70 percent of online users said they saw nothing wrong in online piracy.

22

In 2015, 22 percent of all global internet bandwidth was used for cyber piracy.

95

In 2015, 95 percent of all downloaded music was pirated.

75

In 2015, 75 percent of computers had at least one illegally downloaded application installed.

42

In 2016, 42 percent of all software running around the world was estimated to be pirated.

34.2 billion

In 2016, there were 34.2 billion visits to music piracy sites, and for the first time, mobile pirate site visits overtook desktop ones.

150

Today, around 150 pirate radio stations are thought to still be in operation in the UK.

4 million

The UK Intellectual Property Office's 2017 report on online copyright infringement found 17 percent (4 million) of ebooks read online are pirated. However, if you are reading a pirate copy of this, I don't see how I can complain. Good work, pirate.

Part Three

THE PIRATE CODE

10. ORIGINAL PIRATE MATERIAL

Lock Down Your Aerial

It's show time! This is when you take everything you've learned so far and put it to work. But exactly how are you going to be more pirate in the long shadow of a Monday morning? How will you ever remember whether you're supposed to be Rebelling or Retelling or one of those other Rs? Where is the illustrated flat-pack guide to causing good trouble?

Yet again, Golden Age pirates have the answer, this time in the form of the Pirate Code, which was a sort of immutable manifesto of pirate law. This chapter will draw on original and authentic versions of the code from the Golden Age to inspire you to build your own, a personalized Pirate Code that will help you turn your dreams and schemes into reality. At the end of the next chapter you'll be ready to create your own bespoke code, a Pirate Code 2.0 upgraded for the twenty-first century. With the pirate framework for change behind you, and your very own Pirate Code ahead, soon you will be ready to take on your world and win.

The five stages and chapters we've just worked through replicate the steps that pirates took to create lasting change. However, the pirates' ideas that have inspired us so far, the ones that started out at the edges and went on to permeate mainstream culture, were successful and stood the test of time only because they were enshrined within the Pirate Code.

The Pirate Code is also known as the Pirate Articles, Articles of Association, Code of the Brethren, or Code of the Coast. To keep things straightforward, though, we'll use Pirate Code as the overall term for each set of rules, and "articles" to refer to the individual elements, clauses, or bullet points that made up each code.

Completing the workshop challenge sections at the end of the last few chapters will already have provided you with a few potential articles of your own in development for you to draw on as we examine in depth three authentic eighteenth-century codes in this chapter, and then some great examples of contemporary twenty-first-century codes in the next will inspire you to assemble your personal code. But first, in order to become the architect of your own world-conquering code, it's essential to appreciate how the pirates used theirs.

The Pirate Code has always been part of the pirate story. Throughout the Golden Age, its contents inspired much tap-room gossip and its legendary lore helped make many memoirs of pirate adventure into the bestselling books of the time. It's easy to see why: the radical reorganizing principles of the code were almost seditious, and the sharp references to pirate mischief and misadventure were salacious. It was a winning combination.

When Robert Louis Stevenson's *Treasure Island* was published over one hundred years after the Golden Age of piracy, these infamous piratical principles were subsumed into wider popular culture. The book became the Harry Potter of its day as grown-up tales of good and evil were made into children's adventures. In more recent history, the code was name-checked in the *Pirates of the Caribbean* movies, when Captain Hector Barbossa, played by Geoffrey Rush, inaccurately stated that "the code is more what you'd call guidelines than actual rules." Hollywood once again sells the pirate story short. Make no mistake, "more what you'd call guidelines" these were not. Rules enforced on pain of a frightful death they absolutely were.

The Pirate Code was the backbone of the Golden Age pirates' success. Each code was reformulated afresh at the start of every new mission and also remained remarkably consistent over time. The codes were worked out collaboratively by the crew and enshrined fundamental pirate principles, such as transparent and dynamic pay structures alongside occasionally very specific and bespoke rules such as not smuggling women aboard dressed as men or not getting drunk before tying up prisoners. These and others illustrate a responsive and tactical nature to the code as well as the broader strategic consistent themes.

Often the codes were oral contracts, because written records would have provided cast-iron proof of being a pirate, which was enough to warrant a death sentence. They had to be concise and memorable, and focus laser-like on the essential issues.

The Pirate Code was flexible and fluid yet rigorous and robust. It was a system that created consistency but also allowed for change. Each code was fiercely enforced, but its articles were updated and adapted to accommodate the needs and experience of the individuals who made up the crew. The Pirate Code was mandatory, made by many, bespoke to all. It gave the pirates order amid chaos, rules among the unruly, and trust among the untrustworthy. Not that I'm suggesting any one of you is more untrustworthy, chaotic, or unruly than I am, but the times we're living in most certainly are, and this is why we need a system with flexibility and fluidity, and a structure that will help us navigate the choppy seas ahead.

Living and working by your Pirate Code will help you organize, mobilize, and realize your dreams without sacrificing your ideals or individuality to the collective strength that you need. This is how pirates found fair governance instead of following flawed governments. This is how they kept it light while remaining strong, how they moved so fast but packed such a big punch.

To illustrate the power the pirates harnessed through this somewhat radical operating system, I'm going to present three classic codes for comparison. They are from Henry Morgan, William Kidd, and Bartholomew "Black Bart" Roberts, three legendary pirates whose consecutive adventures span the full forty-year duration of the Golden Age.

Henry Morgan's code from the 1670s kicks off with the core articles we see appearing time and time again across all crews in the subsequent thirty years. His code is a short one with nearly every article containing some element of social justice from fair pay to workplace compensation.

Kidd's code dates from 1696. As a pirate and a privateer, Kidd was infamously untrustworthy, and the detail within each article perhaps shows both his crew's wariness of him and Kidd's desire to assert control.

The code of Bartholomew Roberts from 1722 seems to me particularly poignant as he was sailing after the Pirate Republic had been crushed and many of the most famous pirate heroes killed. Consequently, his code has the scent of the end's being nigh.

Taken as a snapshot together, these three codes demonstrate how their dynamic structure allowed small groups to overcome huge odds and effectively accommodate a wide spectrum of ideals and agendas successfully for half a century.

I have left out the long administrative articles concerning unloading at docks, victuals, wear and tear, etc., etc., which is why the numbering is not consecutive. (And I know you would have skipped them anyway, being the pirate that you are by now.)

Deep Trust Is the Basis for Everything (and Don't Mess with It)

Introducing the Pirate Code of Henry Morgan – 1670 something

Captain Morgan was that rare breakthrough pioneer who achieved mainstream success without selling out. His code became a benchmark for all other pirate crews and was recorded by his frenemy and unofficial biographer, Alexandre Exquemelin, a physician who sailed with Morgan for many years and published *The Buccaneers of America* in 1678, wherein the following is recorded.

THE ARTICLES OF HENRY MORGAN AND OTHER BUCCANEERS—1670s

I. No prey, no pay: "The fund of all payments under the articles is the stock of what is gotten by the expedition, following the same law as other pirates."

III. A standard compensation is provided for maimed and mutilated buccaneers: "Thus they order for the loss of an arm 600 pieces of eight, or six slaves; for a leg 500 pieces of eight, or five slaves; for an eye 100 pieces of eight, or one slave; for a finger of the hand the same reward as for the eye."

IV. Shares of booty are provided as follows: "The Captain, or chief Commander, is allotted five or six portions to what the ordinary seamen have; the Master's Mate only two; and Officers proportionate to their employment. After whom they draw equal parts from the highest even to the lowest mariner, the boys not being omitted."

V. Trust cannot be taken lightly: "In the prizes they take, it is severely prohibited to everyone to usurp anything, in particular to themselves. . . . Yea, they make a solemn oath to each other not to abscond, or conceal the least thing they find amongst the prey. If afterwards any one is found unfaithful, who has contravened the said oath, immediately he is separated and turned out of the society."

Hold up! Before we move on, we have to address the reference to slaves as a form of compensation payment which wholly undermines that otherwise progressive article. In the 1600s, slavery was a massive international, if wholly immoral, commercial operation earning many middle-class families a small fortune. This doesn't excuse the pirates' approach, but it does reveal the inescapably ugly historical context of the day. However, as time passed, after about 1700 when the Golden Age really got under way, the option of payment in slaves disappeared altogether from subsequent codes. Indeed, the number of freed slaves joining pirate crews rose significantly, with equal say and pay for all becoming commonplace.

The fact of pirates' participation in slavery cannot be ignored or erased, but at least their relationship with it evolved and improved over time, and much, much faster than the rest of the "civilized" world. Historians such as Kenneth Kinkor, who argued that "the deck of a pirate ship was the most empowering place for blacks within the eighteenth-century white man's world,"[1] believed that as the Golden Age progressed, so did the pirates' attitudes, evidenced by their regularly freeing slaves and giving them equal say. Marcus Rediker, Colin Woodard, and other prominent pirate historians also lend their weight in this direction. Arne Bialuschewski, on the other hand, cites evidence that human trafficking continued on pirates' watch throughout the Golden Age.[2] Clearly, some pirates were less progressive than others, and no excuses can be made for slavery.

With that acknowledged, let's start unpacking the code to identify which parts will be most useful for you. While the early instance of fair-pay principles, the sliding scale of injury compensation, and the overall equality of the arrangements between members are all striking, the most important point for you to chew over now is the final section of Article V:

> It is severely prohibited to everyone to usurp anything, in particular to themselves. . . . If afterwards any one is found unfaithful, who has contravened the said oath, immediately he is separated and turned out of the society.

All ideas of pirates as anarchic, chaotic, and despotic are buried here forever and for good. At the end of the pirate day, their strength was built on trust, their community was connected through collaboration, and their culture was created safe in the knowledge they had one another's backs and weren't going to prize individual gain over shared values. These communities were such sophisticated systems, with strong bonds and fair rewards, that the worst punishment one could endure was to be removed from them. On such simple ideas do strong societies flourish.

As your ideas turn into adventures, and as your adventures gain a following and a community, governed by your own Pirate Code, you'll know you're successful when remaining in that group becomes motivation enough to keep your team accountable. Business and management guru Peter Drucker once famously said, "Culture eats strategy for breakfast," demonstrating that an organization's success is founded on its shared values and beliefs, not its targets and tactics. The buccaneers who paved the way for the Golden Age of Piracy are early proof of this. If you think of your team as a collective, or even as a society, and the individuals within it as citizens where deep trust is the ultimate currency, then the secret of lasting success is secured and all subsequent strategies will be infinitely more successful.

Enshrine Your Essentials (and Learn from Your Mistakes)

Introducing the Pirate Code of William Kidd—1696

Captain Kidd is among history's best-known pirates, but his true story is a sad and complex affair. World famous when he was on the account, infamous for killing one of his own crew with a bucket (don't ask), he developed a reputation for seeking the odd pardon and passing the buck for his deeds.

Kidd started out as a privateer (the officially sanctioned type of pirate) but quickly switched sides (more than once). When he eventually found himself on trial for piracy, Kidd claimed innocence and blamed the whole thing on his crew (see what I mean about passing the buck?). Some of Kidd's successes were in part due to the backdoor deals he made with senior politicians and the Lords of Trade back in London, who at the time controlled the shipping lanes. As the resentment between the American governors and their colonial masters continued to brew, Kidd unwittingly became a pawn in a *Game of Thrones*-level web of double cross, deception, and disguise that was ultimately his undoing.

Kidd had to watch his back, and his crew had to watch

Kidd, which in part might explain some of the detail in this code, a sort of added protection among pirates, but most interesting to see is the development but also consistency from Morgan's code to Kidd's.

THE ARTICLES OF WILLIAM KIDD—1696[3]

Articles of Agreement concluded upon this tenth day of September Anno Domini 1696 between Captain William Kidd, Commander of the good ship the Adventure Galley, *and John Walker, Quartermaster to the said ship's company, as followeth:*

V. Fair payouts: "That if any man shall lose an eye, leg or arm or the use thereof in the ship or company service, he shall receive as a recompense for the loss thereof 600 pieces of eight or six able slaves to be paid out of the whole stock before any dividend be made." (Again, this clause demonstrates that the more progressive ideals within these articles should not be romanticized or taken out of context of the time.)

VII. Early inheritance act: "That if any man lose his life in time of engagement or by any accident in the ship, or company's service, his share shall be paid to his attorney for the use of his family or friend."

VIII. New business bonus: "That man who shall first see a sayle, if she prove to be a prize, shall receive 100 pieces of eight to be paid out of the whole stock before any dividend be made."

X. The coward clause: "That man that is proved a coward in time of engagement shall lose his share."

XI. The drunkard clause: "That man that shall be drunk in time of engagement before the prisoners then taken be secured, shall lose his share."

XII. No rule breaking among the rule breakers: "That man that shall breed a mutiny or ryot on board the ship shall lose his share, and receive such corporal punishment as the Capt and major part of the company shall think fitt."

XIV. No thievery among the thieves: "That if any man shall defraude the company to the value of one piece of eight shall lose his share and be put on shore upon the first inhabited island or other place."

XV. Swashbuckling socialism: "That what money or treasure shall be taken by the said ship and company shall be put on board of the man of war, and there be shared immediately, and all wares and merchandise to be equally divided amongst the ship's company."

These articles were formulated about two decades after the original code set down by Morgan, with no formal published records or pirate secretariat to maintain a link between the two. There was no WikiPirate available to make a quick check of what the rules were, so pirates needed codes that whole crews could remember. They would have been shared by word of mouth by what were predominantly illiterate pirates, which makes it even more remarkable that so many specific articles retain consistently sharp focus across different crews' codes. The takeaway from this is to focus on the principles that you think are worth preserving over time. Ask yourself what are the fundamentals you'd want your crew to remember verbatim.

While there is an impressive degree of continuity between these codes, at the same time you can see evolution, layers, and added sophistication as the needs of the crew change and lessons are learned from previous adventures and misadventures.

Point XI, for example, which threatens punishment to anyone who gets drunk during "an engagement" (a fight) before any prisoners have been "secured" (tied up or locked away). I mean, that's so specific it's impossible not to imagine that something very bad had happened to demand its inclusion. It sounds to me like the pirates won a fight and, while in the process of taking care of their new prisoners, got so shitfaced that the captives then either escaped or, worse, turned the tables and attacked their captors.

I'm guessing that challenges around drinking, fighting, and tying up your team are not why you're here, but I'm also guessing you've made a mistake or two in your time that you never want to repeat. When your crew gets bigger, you don't want them making the same mistakes as you, so how you help them avoid those pitfalls is all-important. *Hey, guys, let me tell you about the time I was SOOO smashed I couldn't tie up the prisoners and they ended up tying me up!* is not a good look.

It's easy to see from looking at these two codes that the pirates learned from their mistakes and tied up their prisoners before opening the rum, but the major evolution from Morgan's blueprint I want to draw attention to is the idea that friend or family can receive social compensation for those killed in action. If such considerate, compassionate inheritance arrangements don't sound like the pirates we've grown up hearing about, then remember matelotage—pirates' same-sex "marriages." Clearly, the pirates formed relationships with each other sufficiently close that they warranted an inheritance clause.

Tight-knit communities that rely on one another for survival need to trust one another implicitly and feel safe in the knowledge that they will look after one another when seas get rough. When it comes to building a team or a following, take time to consider the incentives, the rewards, and the reassurances you build into your community. If you really listen to what matters to you and your team and provide it, you'll build deep and powerful motivation, trust, and appreciation well beyond the essential but transactional incentives of pay, promotion, and pensions.

Go Hard on Your Values (and Don't Forget the Band)

Introducing the Pirate Code of Bartholomew Roberts—1722

Bartholomew "Black Bart" Roberts, aka Black Barty, aka Barti Ddu (Bart's Welsh name), was sailing the high seas some forty years after the original code was laid down by Morgan.

His code is remarkable for two things in particular. First,

the essentials have been not only maintained but also given razor-sharp focus; the very first article is a clear statement of total equality in both reward received and decision-making power.

Second, Bart's code shows a real sensitivity to the ever-shifting needs of a specific mission. We see, as with Kidd's code, that the pirates learned from their previous mistakes and adapted the code to refine their values while voyaging, in this case with a ban on gambling.

THE ARTICLES OF BARTHOLOMEW ROBERTS, FEBRUARY 1722[4]

I. Every man has a vote in affairs of moment; has equal title to the fresh provisions, or strong liquors, at any time seized, and may use them at pleasure, unless a scarcity makes it necessary, for the good of all, to vote a retrenchment.

II. Every man to be called fairly in turn, by list, on board of prizes because (over and above their proper share) they were on these occasions allowed a shift of clothes: but if they defrauded the company to the value of a dollar in plate, jewels, or money, marooning was their punishment.

III. No person to game at cards or dice for money.

IV. The lights and candles to be put out at eight o'clock at night: if any of the crew after that hour still remained inclined for drinking, they were to do it on the open deck.

VI. No woman to be allowed amongst them. If any man were to be found seducing any of the latter sex, and carried her to sea, disguised, he was to suffer death.

VIII. No striking one another on board, but every man's quarrels to be ended on shore, at sword and pistol.

IX. No man to talk of breaking up their way of living, till each had shared one thousand pounds. If in order to this, any man should lose a limb, or become a cripple in their service, he was to have eight hundred dollars, out of the public stock, and for lesser hurts, proportionately.

X. The captain and quartermaster to receive two shares of a prize: the master, boatswain, and gunner, one share and a half, and other officers one and a quarter.

XI. The musicians to have rest on the Sabbath Day, but the other six days and nights, none without special favour.

Over forty years after Captain Morgan inspired the Pirate Code, Bartholomew Roberts keeps the faith with such an impressive degree of diligence and consistency on the big issues like fair pay, a clear system of social insurance, and participatory and representative democratic decision-making.

And then these prescient parts of the Pirate Code that appear across multiple crews and many decades are accompanied by articles so very specific as to almost feel random. But they nonetheless demonstrate that the power of the Pirate Code was its ability to cover simultaneously both big issues and the all-important detail.

Article VI makes clear the threat of death for mistreating or "carrying to sea" any woman, especially one dressed in men's clothing. By most accounts, pirate ships were predominantly male environments, sometimes progressively so, as we've seen with the instance of a same-sex civil ceremony, and sometimes the norm was broken by legends like Anne Bonny and Mary Read. But on the whole, women on board were a rarity and therefore provision for their treatment must have been occasionally essential. Some pirates liked to show off their gentlemanly credentials with the good treatment of their female captives, and also some real horror stories exist. It is therefore interesting to see a clause in protection of women in this instance, although it is a rare one, and like the other articles we've looked at, it was probably put in place to overcome previous problems on board.

The last article is also worth a moment of your time: to see, among all these detailed articles about robbing, sharing stolen goods, and accountability held through violence, (a) that Black Bart gave the band a break on Sundays and (b) the fact that Black Bart had a band. An actual band on a pirate ship. Playing six days a week? See what I mean about poignant?

I know that was a lot of sometimes torturously seventeenth-century language where any person that shall have to read of such a thing may have to read of it two times or more to know what such thing meant in the first place. Sorry about that. But I wanted you to be able to taste the blood, sweat, and salt of the real-deal authentic and surviving Pirate Code in all of its wordy glory.

Confusing yet consistent, progressive yet prejudiced,

fair but fierce, the Pirate Code is a fascinating reflection of the times. It's worth an investigation all of its own, and there is a lot written about it, but if you're interested to find out more I would specifically point to E. T. Fox's dissertation "'Piratical Schemes and Contracts': Pirate Articles and Their Society, 1660–1730" for a robust examination and a deeper critique of some of the potentially progressive interpretations of the code.[5]

For our purposes, though, once again, we're accepting that there is moral relativity between the Golden Age and the modern age, and trying to draw out the strategic lessons relevant to surviving in uncertainty and sailing into uncharted horizons, and in that, the Pirate Code holds many useful attributes. It successfully held a crew to account, it successfully allowed dynamic structures, it ensured democratic principles were enshrined, and at the most positive and profound end of its impact, its influence can be felt in a number of movements and moments across history when humanity has taken a real step forward.

From Codes to Cooperatives

We've seen how Pirate Codes developed over a span of forty years, and at many points in this book we've looked at the profound impact that pirates' policies had on the world. Many pirate historians and economists have pointed to the commonality between some of the pirates' innovative and progressive practices and social developments that occur later in mainstream civilization—for example, the implementation of workplace insurance. They've argued that Captain Henry Morgan's was the first use of a compensation payout, long before the Employers' Liability Act that came into law in the UK in 1880. Some even point out that the pirates' approach to compensation is further mirrored in Article 22 of the 1948 UN Universal Declaration of Human Rights that states, "Everyone, as a member of society, has the right to social security," some 250 years after every pirate citizen assumed the same right, signed up to in blood in their Pirate Code. But the pirates weren't intent on creating principles that would one day become inalienable human rights; they were generating clear, simple rules that would make their own lives fairer.

We could spend a long time looking at each article across all the Pirate Codes, tracing its influence over time, illustrating how ideas born on a pirate ship went on to permeate the mainstream so profoundly that they sparked particular social reforms, but there are such things as editors, word counts, and your attention span to consider. If you'd like to dive deeper and learn more on the subject then I highly recommend you listen to the Pirate History Podcast that I've already mentioned, or go to www.bemorepirate.com, where there are all manner of links and articles on the influence individual Pirate Codes have had on society.

But there is one such link that I've uncovered that I think is worth sharing with you here, because it's a point I don't think has ever been made anywhere else. Informed by my perspective as a social entrepreneur, pioneering change from the edges of capitalism, I was inspired by the idea of pirates as metaphor, but as I spent more time deep in the many sets of secondary sources, learning about their history and in particular the Pirate Code, I came to realize that piracy is not just a metaphor for mission-led businesses and social enterprises, it's a bloodline. Way back, long before they were social enterprises, the original purpose-driven business model was the cooperative movement, and from what I can see, before there was the cooperative movement, there were pirates.

Most people are aware of the cooperative principle, whereby the employees of a company are also its owners. Most people are not aware of how many of these companies exist, or the extent to which their founding principles are borrowed from the Golden Age pirates.

From humble beginnings in the early 1800s on the west coast of England, Scotland, and Wales, the movement now operates across all major sectors in every global economy and is worth about $20 trillion.[6] The founding father of the movement was Robert Owens, a Welsh textile manufacturer who dedicated his life to improving the conditions of his factory workers and developing and promoting a form of socialism. Owens was born just a few miles from Henry Morgan's birthplace in Wales, a country that was also home to so many of the other pirate legends from Henry Avery to Bartholomew Roberts, whose stories and success would have been well known throughout such a small and close-knit country.

At the end of the Golden Age, when many pirates returned home to England, they found the Industrial Revolution in full swing, with England's "dark satanic mills" offering the same sort of working conditions they'd suffered in the navy a generation before. The idea that workers could defend their rights or attempt any form of shared ownership was considered revolutionary by those in power and carried the threat of punishment. The returning swashbucklers were met once again with a broken and abusive establishment, but this time they had stories to share with local workers about an inspiring, authentic, and credible alternative.

Morgan and the other pirate legends would have been working-class local heroes in the small Welsh communities they came from, and the ideals Morgan pioneered and sailed under would have been well known to those who lived close by. It's hard to imagine that their more progressive principles wouldn't have captured the imagination of the oppressed workers back home when they had been ubiquitous among sailors the world over, and hard to believe Robert Owens wouldn't have been aware of, and indeed influenced by, Morgan's and other pirates' principles. If we look at the seven founding principles of the cooperative movement it's not difficult to see the similarity between them and the Pirate Codes:

1. Voluntary and open membership—Everyone is welcome to join the alternative society.
2. Democratic member control—Everyone gets a fair say.
3. Member economic participation—Everyone gets a fair share.
4. Autonomy and independence—Free from authority, controlled by their members.
5. Education and training—Everyone is encouraged to work effectively together.
6. Cooperation among cooperatives—Scale is achieved through their network.
7. Concern for the community—Everyone is looked after.

Given the extreme similarity in principles and the proximity of location between Owens's, Morgan's, and so many of the best-known pirates' hometowns, I don't think it's any coincidence that the cooperatives' code is so closely aligned with those of the Golden Age pirates; it seems to be clearly inspired by them.

Excited to have made this discovery, but concerned not to overstate myself, I spoke to Gillian Lonergan, the librarian at the Co-operative Heritage Trust and National Co-operative Archive, who's heard the comparison before. As she said, "The equality, collaboration, and standing up against the status quo are all obvious connections."

Gillian also helped me find the missing link I was looking for. The principles are the same, but the approach to their implementation differed vastly: pirates create change through conflict, while cooperatives achieve their goals through, well, cooperating.

In addition, she gave me a missing part of the story: at sea, the radical reorganizing principles of the pirates had become the norm, but back on land they could get you arrested, if not executed. The early cooperatives were inherently peaceful movements, but that doesn't make them any less radical than their predecessors, as Gillian told me:

> One factor that has always seemed important to me is the timing of the cooperative movement. It developed at a time when the British government was seriously concerned that the British population would follow France into violent revolution and upheaval. When the Fenwick Weavers [the earliest documented cooperative society] held their meetings

in the 1760s, working people were actively discouraged from gathering for meetings, so they held them outdoors, by a wall at a place where five roads met, so that if official intervention came, they could scatter.

The pirates brought back more than gold when they returned to England; they returned with interesting ideas that went on to inspire and influence future generations. They sought solutions to their problems, coming up with alternatives that would make their own lives better, and ended up changing the lives of so many more people as a consequence. Their ideas changed society, and so can yours. Now, fascinating diversions into working-class history aside, it's time to get back to the point of the whole thing.

The Point of the Whole Thing

The Pirate Code allowed pirates to agree upon the shared values and rules of their community in a clear and easy-to-follow way. The pirates knew what was expected of them and what punishment they would receive if they went rogue, as they all played a part in creating and signing off on the articles. They used their code to ensure their missions were a success, and they made sure to update and adapt them to prevent them from becoming redundant, limiting, or outdated.

Here we are, some three hundred years later, championing the need for agile networks, facilitative leadership, person-centric organizations and other buzzwords. Most of our organizations are addicted to pointless policy. Our suffocating environment can't escape the choke hold of a global economy that depends on it. In far too many cases, politics, business, and society go around in circles in terms of procedures and process, designed to help us but that might actually harm us.

We've allowed ourselves to become convinced that there is no alternative to the systems, processes, and rules we've been given and that this is as good as it gets, even when it's obvious that it's always the same people who suffer and the same people who win or lose. We often shrug and accept that those are the rules.

But pirates don't.

By rewriting the rules and creating a code, these eighteenth-century pirates, whom we once believed were all mayhem, booty, and timber shivering, turned their dissatisfaction and rebellion into a sophisticated societal structure that changed the course of history. They proved you can create alternatives—that a small group can opt out and start something new—and their ideas eventually influenced the mainstream. This really is the point of the whole thing. Their code never mutated into a painful bureaucratic policy that held them back, because they continually updated it, stress-testing it to make sure it was working for them and offering better alternatives when it wasn't. The Pirate Code is robust yet flexible, strict yet adaptive, accessible and simple yet sophisticated, and can be just as effective now as it was three centuries ago at accommodating ambitious agendas, egos, and ideals while also protecting, testing, and expanding good ideas to allow them to become great ideas.

The code you create will not suffocate decision-making or stifle creativity like so many organizations' and authorities' policies tend to. Your code will keep you moving with the times and provide a blueprint for your road to success. You've learned how a code can guide adventure, preserve ideals, and compound good ideas; now it's time to go back to the future and look at some modern pirate articles that you can steal in the creation of your own code. Your Pirate Code 2.0 awaits.

11. THE PIRATE CODE 2.0

Steal Like an Artist

By the end of this chapter you will have the beginnings of your own Pirate Code that you can add to and adapt as you see fit, mission by mission, side hustle by side hustle, and adventure by adventure. You will have a basic but bespoke framework for your own Pirate Code—a whole new way of getting things done, a guide to making clearer, faster, and better decisions based on what really matters to you and your crew.

When exciting opportunities and death-defying deadlines rush toward you, your code will allow you to stay calm and clearheaded as they whoosh overhead and into view. When the rules of the game change, and not in your favor, leaving you without time to think, your code will help you remain responsive while also holding firm to your course. When your to-do list ties knots in your abdomen and your inbox makes you want to scream at your screen, your code will help you cut through the crap and get directly to the gold.

And don't worry. The first steps to creating your Pirate Code are very simple. A successful Pirate Code is all about adoption and adaptation, choosing and cherry-picking which articles might work for you. In other words, you're going to start by stealing someone else's.

In the spirit of being more pirate, I've stolen some other

people's articles for you to steal from me. When it comes to creating a code that's going to help you change your world, in true pirate fashion, steal anything and everything that works for you. As the legendary filmmaker Jim Jarmusch is widely quoted as saying, "Nothing is original. Steal from anywhere that resonates with inspiration or fuels your imagination. Select only things to steal from that speak directly to your soul. If you do this, your work (and theft) will be authentic. Authenticity is invaluable; originality is nonexistent."

Just make sure that when you do steal, you always steal the best, and try to make sure you stay on the right side of stealing so you don't wind up with a criminal record.

Looking to a wide range of modern pirates for inspiration, I have pirated the very best for you, creating a source code that I'd be happy to live, work, and die by, and that hopefully you'll find something you can draw from. I'm very lucky to spend time in the space between business, policy, entrepreneurship, and social change; it's an intersection that sees some of the world's best solution-focused innovative, imaginative, and impactful individuals, organizations, and ideas. This is where I've sourced my suggested starter articles from that you can use for the foundations of your code, choosing to save or scrap any of the ones I'm about to present.

When it comes to big ideas, it might not always be apparent or even important how big the potential consequence of the idea is, only that it's a big deal for us, for you, for now. As we've seen, for the pirates being paid fairly, for instance, seemed like a great idea for them; they didn't think they were starting a fair pay debate that would last three hundred years. In much the same way, being compensated if you were injured felt like the right thing to do for their democratic community, though they probably didn't imagine it was going to become a human right a few centuries later. Like the pirates, we don't need to worry about creating articles that will stand the test of time and change the world. We just need the ideas to work for you now, and following the paradox of scale, the right ideas made to work really well for a small group might just become those that end up having an impact on everything. The codes protected the integrity of the pirates' ideas, kept them authentic as they lived them, and ensured that even over decades, they held true to their intentions, while their ideas compounded and eventually took hold at a much broader level. Big ideas, small steps. Take what works, make it work for you, and watch it fly.

Victor Hugo, one of the greatest French writers of all time and author of *Les Misérables*, the world's best-known depiction of the French Revolution, was a firm believer in the unstoppable force of human progress. While in exile from France under Napoleon, he observed: "There is one thing stronger than all the armies in the world, and that is an idea whose time has come and hour has struck." I held this thought in mind as my benchmark when I sourced the following articles for you—I was looking for ideas whose hour had come, and that one day could compound as far as the pirates have.

At the end of the chapter I'll show you how to assemble your set of articles to create your code, but for now, sit back and take in the codes I've selected for you. As you read each suggested article, consider the following questions to decide whether you should include it in your own Pirate Code 2.0:

Does this article reflect values I respect? Can it give me an edge against my rivals? Could it help me make better decisions? How would I feel if I knew the rest of my crew were living by it? And last, possibly most important, does it, or part of it, really excite me? If no, move along; if yes or partly yes, steal with glee.

Stolen Goods:

Introducing the Articles of Sam Conniff Allende's Pirate Code 2.0—2018

Article 1—Make Shit Up

THE CHALLENGE

We need to get good at making things up responsibly, immediately, and decisively. If we're going to keep up with the unpredictability that regularly outpaces us, we need license for mature but in-the-moment application of imagination. We need to reduce an overwhelming reliance on chain-of-command thinking, a dangerous default to data-always-knows-best, risk-averse, and rule book decision-making, and empower individuals within all our organizations to try stuff out in the search for new answers to old problems. We need to be clear about the differences between being fake and being fast.

When the truth is that no one knows what's coming next, there is danger in relying on rules that were made for a time that's been. We need to think on our feet and for ourselves, to critically assess what's "right" when things change, and to know when not to follow the crowd or tolerate lies.

We need to evolve the notion of a feeling in our gut from sounding like some sort of last-ditch reassurance, to recognize that in an experienced individual a sharpened and honed instinct is among our most valuable resources.

Just as we've come to terms with the idea of emotional intelligence and the importance of empathy within organizations, so too do we need to recognize the significance of intuition, another easily overlooked "softer" skill that when carefully applied can provide a consistent edge to decision-making.

We need to be able to look each other in the eyes and admit that more often than not, we're making it up most of the time anyway, so we should collaborate and make it up better together.

SUGGESTED ARTICLE

All captains and crews profoundly expect, respect, celebrate, and appreciate the art of strategically, structurally, intuitively, and instantly making shit up. Not irresponsible imaginings, reckless reimaginings, *and certainly not false or fake news. We champion creative solution finding and positive problem solving based on available facts, the moment of opportunity, and the power of practiced intuition. When indecision is not an option, when change is constant and nothing is normal, we're proudly comfortable to rationally and rapidly develop, test, and implement solutions on the spot. We learn from our mistakes, even if we don't celebrate them, and use them to make making it up better.*

INSPIRATION

The idea that failing is a positive thing has gained more traction in recent years. How can you argue with Google's law of failure, the understanding that nine out of ten ideas fail, so if we fail faster we get to the good idea quicker? I, like many other people, really bought into this idea. Fail fast, fail better. It felt cool, a bit edgy, and was a great line to throw into a conversation, presentation, or pitch deck.

Only it didn't come true. No one really likes failing, and very few people have the real nerve to celebrate it. So once we tired of the cool posters, it began to feel incredibly disingenuous. The nail in the coffin for me came at a leadership retreat for one of the world's biggest companies that was facing disruption on every side and striving for innovation within. I was speaking to their "fast track" talent at a three-day retreat and providing stimulus to drive more innovative thinking and working. One of the up-and-coming execs, a super-sharp future leader of the organization with groundbreaking ideas, held the most senior people in the business to account on this very point. "Okay," he said, "I've got lots of ideas and can see solutions you can't. I'm grateful to be in this position, but can you give me your assurance that I can put my ideas into practice and fail nine times and still keep my job and your support all the way to my tenth idea and success?"

Of course they could not, so he took his ideas and left. Those ideas were revolutionary and will be industry changing when he finds a home for them. The company in question remains one of the top fifty in the world, but has just posted profit warnings. Again.

The Pretotyping Manifesto, which we touched on earlier in Chapter 5, is a very helpful approach that enables anyone to make something up, test it out, and create a conversation around an idea that might just help bring it to life. Pretotyping is the stage before prototyping, which used to be the thing you did first but now, thanks to Alberto Savoia, the man who came up with Google's law of failure, there's this even earlier stage that allows a safe space for making shit up as the first stage of making shit happen.

Savoia asks you to ask yourself what's the version of your

idea you can make for no or low cost, on your phone or with paper and pens. Take a look at the manifesto for inspiration, not least to find out how a broken chopstick and piece of wood can test an idea that revolutionized technology without costing a penny.

The point is to create a pretotype model so that you can see what it looks like, feels like, and might be like. It's smart, fast, fun, and anybody can apply it. I suggest you do, often. For more on this, visit www.pretotyping.org/.

WARNING

The art of making shit up has an emphasis on the "making": making it happen, making it real, faking it until you make it, etc., and this is where the article really aligns with the principles of pretotyping, encouraging you to grab any of thousands of free online tools and platforms and see what your ideas look like when you make them up.

- If you want to see if a product concept will find an audience, but can't afford the research and development, mock up a Kickstarter campaign or take a look at any crowdfunding site; you might find an audience and the funding you need to make it happen.

- If you have an idea that needs a community to form around it in order to get going, try writing it up and putting it on Eventbrite or Meetup, even if it's only for a handful of people or even to see how it looks.

- If you're thinking about running a campaign, why not test an online petition, set a target, and see if you can beat it, whether it's ten or ten thousand signatures.

- If you're not sure if your idea is strong enough to be a real company, spend a few hours and mock up a couple of website pages using templates on WordPress or Squarespace, and see what it looks like, how it feels, and test it out on some friends.

Article 2—Business Plans Are Dead

THE CHALLENGE

We need a more fluid and flexible way of setting out our hopes, ideas, and dreams and a more motivating way to manage and measure ourselves to achieve those dreams than the anachronistic, static (and if we're really honest, often ignored) "business plan" allows.

The ubiquitous "business plan" format has overstayed its welcome. Created over a hundred years ago, its template has stagnated, whereas what "business" means, how it looks, and its relationship with the economy, society, the environment, and the individual have transformed. But the blueprint, with its intrinsic old-world tactics, is still the default response to anyone with a big idea that they want others to take seriously, even if "business" as a term no longer does justice to the diversity of your creativity, to your hustle, to your ideas or ambitions.

Of course, there is still a need to assess the opportunities for your ideas to flourish in the future and create responsible growth plans and protect them, but there is also a need to do so just as fluidly as the environment in which you are operating is changing.

SUGGESTED ARTICLE

We challenge a century-old static format as the best structure for the fluid future of our organizations, projects, dreams, and schemes. We believe in a motivating manifesto that makes clear our vision, and we follow a concise but responsive road map with agile measures of accountability. We believe in collaborative "working" and adaptive formats that are regularly used and reviewed in collaboration with not just the whole crew but even our customers, beneficiaries, and stakeholders, to openly evaluate success, failure, and future scenario planning. No captain will produce a "plan" for only a narrow audience or a moment in time, only for it to gather dust in an inbox, ignored or unused by the crew.

INSPIRATION

I have long suspected that the process of business planning is subconsciously a mutually agreed act of self-deception between the writer and the reader. I've known countless young people whose ideas defy their older and "wiser" investors' and mentors' imaginations and who literally have to lie through their teeth to satisfy grown-up demands for reliable predictions in what we all know to be unreliable environments and times. These young people, with their strong, curiosity-driven unformed ideas about how to redefine the future, are given the

limiting, twentieth-century template of a "business plan" to help them shape (suffocate) their ideas into a format that older (less imaginative) experts can get their head around.

With this in mind, I asked a group of young social entrepreneurs who are at the cutting edge of innovation, the type of young people I think of as modern-day pirates, what their approach to "business planning" is. Lots of responses included technologies like Trello, Telegram, or Slack, where a plan is more like a thread of conversation, evolving beneath a shared vision, that can be edited and improved as it evolves.

But it's the overall approach that's important, not the tool you use to execute it, which was made clear for me when I heard the challenge "Business plans, Granddad?" from a young social entrepreneur who then educated me in "Manifesto Jams," where "dudes with ideas get together to jam their manifesto" to ensure it gives their crews the motivation and decision-making framework they deserve and need.

Manifesto Jams.

Granddad.

Busted.

The people at the leading edge of this conversation are responsive.org. They have an amazing Slack group you can join to help shape their evolving and electrifying thinking. Here's how they describe themselves, from their own manifesto:

Most organizations still rely on a way of working designed over 100 years ago. . . .

The tension between organizations optimized for predictability and the unpredictable world they inhabit has reached breaking point. . . . Workers caught between dissatisfied customers and uninspiring leaders are becoming disillusioned and disengaged. Executives caught between dis-

contented investors and disruptive competitors are struggling to find a path forward. And people who want a better world for themselves and their communities are looking to new ambitious organizations to shape our collective future.

We need a new way.

There's a reason we've run organizations the way we have. Our old Command and Control operating model was well suited for complicated and predictable challenges. Some of these challenges still exist today and may respond to the industrial-era practices that we know so well. However, as the pace of change accelerates, the challenges we face are becoming less and less predictable. Those practices that were so successful in the past are counterproductive in less predictable environments. In contrast, Responsive Organizations are designed to thrive in less predictable environments by balancing the following tensions:

More Predictable › Less Predictable
Profit › Purpose
Hierarchies › Networks
Controlling › Empowering
Planning › Experimentation
Privacy › Transparency

WARNING

Business plans are not yet extinct, so at some point you will be asked for one, and you'll need to show something to investors, banks, or anyone else trying to work out whether they can take you seriously. The best advice I've had is to keep a plan as short and as honest and as close to a reflection of your genuine vision as you can. Create it in as much collaboration as you can, with the team and ideally even with your target audience and other trusted stakeholders. Do not let it become an exercise in convincing someone else to believe in it. Avoid the three main risks of conventional "business planning":

- Stifling the magic and unquantifiable energy of your idea by forcing it into someone else's template.
- Creating a plan that is out-of-date in three weeks (if you're lucky) because something more interesting and relevant came along.
- Losing touch with your crew, customers, culture, and reality because you're falling into an existential crisis loop aka business planning.

If you want to get to the core of what your plan or manifesto should be so that you can "jam" it in the most direct manner, then pick up a book called *Start with Why* by Simon Sinek—or, if you're short for time, watch his TED Talk (the third most viewed TED Talk of all time).[1] Read/watch it and you'll come back with such clarity of purpose you'll be unbeatable and be able to replace flaky forecasts attempting to predict the unpredictable with bulletproof reasons why you do what you do and a clear and compelling core to build your success on.

Article 3—Make the Citizen Shift

THE CHALLENGE

We need to improve our individual and collective relationships with the world and its natural limitations. We need to develop from an unquestioning consumer mind-set to one where we question, demand, and understand the impact of our choices.

Consumer has become the definition of not just who but what we are. It is a descriptive and prescriptive term for humanity allegedly at its peak.

Once, long ago, we were all "subjects" in service to our rulers. This idea defined who we were in society for centuries and was really upgraded only in the twentieth century when we evolved into "consumers." Consumer thinking has since dominated in the developed world, and as consumers, we have become the passengers of capitalism, fueling its engines and creating decades of growth and a valid belief in the benefits of mass globalization. Consumerism, however, has now passed its sell-by date.

Branding ourselves as consumers is a clear sign we are no longer in charge, but instead are subservient to short-term and self-interested goals, drawn from limited options that are seemingly on special offer.

At a macro level, the principle of the consumer no longer fits in a world that's so far over its capacity—the one-way relationship of consumption has a limited life expectancy.

On a micro and individual level, social experiments that stimulate a "consumer mind-set" in participants have proven that even the single use of the word *consumer* can prompt reactions that are more selfish, less open to participation, and less motivated by environmental concerns.

As billions more of the global population enter a consumer mind-set of middle-class aspiration, and we accelerate past a planetary point of no return in a system based precariously on debt we can't afford and in a world without resources to sustain us, there's a chance the clue to survival is in how we perceive ourselves and the relationship we have with our planet and one another, and it just so happens that the name *consumer* may well be the signature on humanity's suicide note.

SUGGESTED ARTICLE

It's time to evolve the human race beyond the mind-set of solely a "consumer" and the dangerous, destructive, and limited relationships it has created. We will perform a forced reset on the language of consumerism that in turn will help us to develop more interesting, involved, interactive, mutually respectful, and naturally more beneficial, respectful, and rewarding relationships between our organizations, our audiences, and the finite resources of our world. All pirates undertake to advance the evolution of the idea of the citizen as the dominant defining thought of our audiences and communities, and of our future.

INSPIRATION

Founding partners of the New Citizenship Project, Jon Alexander and Irenie Ekkeshis, are both former advertising executives who've done their time in the engine room of consumerism and are now pioneering an alternative idea, that it's time to make the Citizen Shift, where the principles of citizenship replace those of consumerism.

Jon and Irenie are pragmatic, professional, and potentially the smart strategic intervention that's required in an otherwise seemingly insurmountable challenge of the human race eating itself.

The New Citizenship Project presents an optimistic vision that while consumerism had its benefits, if we are to now escape its toxic and limiting relationship with a world of finite and diminishing resources, we need to evolve into citizens. The vision of the New Citizenship Project is that instead of seeing the term *consumer* over a thousand times a day (as most of us do), we replace this with the language of citizen, and in doing so reverse the tyranny of the holy trinity of scale, growth, and consumption. Or as Jon concludes:

You can start, in your own life and work, by changing your language; and you will discover a whole new world. Thinking of people as consumers, the only ideas you can possibly come up with are for stuff people can buy from you; your brain is build-

SUBJECT, CONSUMER, CITIZEN:
QUICKFIRE CONCEPTS

SUBJECT	CONSUMER	CITIZEN
DEPENDENT	INDEPENDENT	INTERDEPENDENT
TO	FOR	WITH
RELIGIOUS	MATERIAL	SPIRITUAL
DUTY	RIGHTS	PURPOSE
OBEY	DEMAND	PARTICIPATE
RECEIVE	CHOOSE	CREATE
COMMAND	SERVE	FACILITATE
PRINT	ANALOGUE	DIGITAL
HIERARCHY	BUREAUCRACY	NETWORK
SUBJECTIVE	OBJECTIVE	DELIBERATIVE

ing on scaffolding that will allow nothing else. But think of people as citizens, and you must start by asking what the purpose of your organization is, and how you could invite people to participate in that purpose. You will move from "us" and "them" to "we." You'll start to create the future. And you'll stop propping up a past that needs to die.[2]

WARNING

Anything deemed anti-consumerism can have a polarizing effect, and there are staunch defenders of the benefits of globalization with good arguments that deserve to be heard and learned from.

Don't let an idea this important get distracted by that debate; don't mistake, or let others mistake, the argument for a move to a citizen mind-set as anything less than a rational case for an evolution, for the next stage in our development and the deepening of our relationships between individuals, organizations, and environment.

One look at the chart on the previous page, taken from the New Citizenship Project's report "The Citizen Shift," will help you navigate this evolution.[3] It's a summary of "quickfire concepts" showing the shift from subject to consumer to citizen.

Article 4—Take Happiness Seriously

THE CHALLENGE

Humanity is experiencing its highest ever-recorded rates of anxiety, depression, and suicide. In the UK and US, depression is at an all-time high. Overexposure to social media and relentless bombardment from advertising and media telling us who and how we should be are all endlessly undermining our already fragile self-worth. And yet while we know a servile relationship to technology, brands, and consumerism makes us sad, we still wake up, check our phones, and follow the call to buy stuff, like stuff, and swipe stuff in order to get an ever-reducing hit of endorphins. According to the 2017 global mobile consumer survey, checking social media is the very first thing many of us do every day, even before we get out of bed.[4] And this would be at least our own fault if we were only semiconsciously doing it to ourselves; it's when you look at the sadness we're systemizing into children's lives it gets really depressing. For example (and there are many examples to choose from): 50 percent of five-year-old girls in the United States worry about their weight, largely inspired by the 3,000 ads they see every day according to a program participated in by Harvard University and led by Jean Kilbourne, the woman behind *Killing Us Softly*. "Women and girls compare themselves to these images every day," Kilbourne said. "And failure to live up to them is inevitable because they are based on a flawlessness that doesn't exist."[5]

In addition to the pervasive nature of advertising, the landscape undermining our happiness has been added to and accelerated by technology. The more time children spend chatting on social media, the less happy they feel about their schoolwork, the school they attend, their appearance, their family, and their life overall, according to a team of economists at the University of Sheffield.[6]

Ever since the need for it led to the advent of World Mental Health Day in the nineties, there is at last a more mature global conversation happening about mental health, well-being, and happiness, but some of it needs to be treated with caution. Because ironically, many of the same brands and sometimes entire industries who made a fortune undermining our self-image are now heavily invested in celebrating our identity. As with any emerging market, there's an app for that, yet for the thousands of well-being apps on the market, according to research published in the journal *Evidence Based Mental Health*, there is no proof that 85 percent of the apps accredited by the National Health Service in the UK actually work.[7] Apps are just the tip of the iceberg, and the once outlying well-being industry has come in from hugs and herbal teas to become a sophisticated multibillion-dollar empire of hermetically packaged lifestyle products.

Even now that we can make some money out of it—which, let's face it, is usually when we begin to consider that something is important—we're still a long way away from taking happiness as seriously as we should.

SUGGESTED ARTICLE

We take happiness seriously, and give deep happiness the place and impor-tance it deserves. We see happiness as a strategic driver for success, productivity, and creative output, but also as a strategic objective in and of itself. We do not believe happiness is a nice-to-have; we believe it is a need-to-have. We make happiness a starting point, not just an end point; we use our intention to achieve happiness to inform the decisions we make, the environments we create, and the projects we undertake. We endeavor to measure, manage, and share the proof we accumulate that happiness is symbiotic with great work, great impact, great relationships, and greater effectiveness. We do not conform to a one-size-fits-all happiness, nor expect to be happy every day, but accept and respect the right to make happiness the goal.

INSPIRATION

There have been several attempts to give happiness the status it deserves. The macroeconomic argument that we should try to measure a country's Gross Domestic Happiness instead of its Gross Domestic Product was first put forward by the king of Bhutan, who coined the phrase, but while popular for a spell with some world leaders, including David "Kiss of Death" Cameron, as an idea it was riven with complexity, and even Bhutan is said to be focusing on more traditional metrics to measure a country's performance.

A 700-person experiment conducted in 2017 in Britain by the Social Market Foundation and the University of Warwick's Centre for Competitive Advantage in the Global Economy provided concrete evidence that happier employees are more productive in the workplace. In the experiment, when happiness metrics were increased, then productivity increased on average by 12 percent, and reached as high as 20 percent. Dr. Daniel Sgroi, the author of the experiment, points out that rises of 3 percent in the comparative GDP are "considered very large."[8]

The researchers also demonstrated a link between unhappiness and decreased productivity that lasted up to two years.

Dr. Sgroi hopes his work will: "Help managers to justify workpractices aimed at boosting happiness on productivity grounds," because, sadly, we couldn't justify them on happiness grounds.

On an individual level, an excellent exploration of the topic (and book) is *Happiness by Design*, by Paul Dolan, a professor of behavioural science at the London School of Economics.[9] Dolan does his own research into happiness: how it happens, how it can be measured, and how it affects us. He moves the debate on significantly from self-help, pop psychology, and mindfulness into a very practical framework as he shows that happiness is not just how you feel, it's how you act and very much what you do. Being happier means we have to look at what's around us, from eliminating the things we waste time on to increasing time spent in nature or with good friends.

There are literally thousands more explorations into not just how we find happiness, but how we embed it into our lives and defend it from being seen as an afterthought, from a multitude of books that range from *The Happiness Project* and *The Architecture of Happiness* to *The Happiness Advantage*, which are all well worth a read. But if you want something more digestible, a search for *happy* at Ted.com will unearth over 500 talks for you, or try SlideShare, where the same search will yield over half a million results.

Clearly, there's no shortage of inspiration. One opportunity that feels genuinely new is a massive open online course being run by University of California at Berkeley on the science of happiness,[10] and claiming to be the first MOOC to teach positive psychology. Learn science-based principles and practices for a happy, meaningful life. The course launches in 2018. I have just signed up.

WARNING

If we are going to get serious about happiness, we also can't get too simplistic. Emily Esfahani Smith, the author of *The Power of Meaning*, warns in a TED Talk against a one-dimensional understanding of happiness and shows that chasing happiness can actually make people more unhappy.[11]

She puts forward a different way, based on four pillars—belonging, purpose, transcendence, and storytelling—to create a "meaningful" life. Taking sides with the Buddhist ideal that "all emotions are useful," Emily makes the case for a meaningful life, which will ultimately make us "happier" rather than being obsessed about happiness.

Multiple heavyweight research institutes, including Harvard's Department of Psychology's longitudinal Study of Adult Development, which followed its subjects for over fifty years, unreservedly agree that relationships are essential, with the happiest (and healthiest) of us being those who cultivated strong relationships with people they trusted to support them.[12]

But don't make the mistake of thinking that because you've got more than the average friends on Facebook (200) or followers on Instagram (150), happiness awaits. Think again, because rigorous research conducted in 2017 confirmed that "the more you use Facebook, the worse you feel."[13] In the *Harvard Business Review* article that reported this, the researchers were quoted as saying:

Our results showed that, while real-world social networks were positively associated with overall well-being, the use of Facebook was negatively associated with overall well-being. These results were particularly strong for men-

tal health; most measures of Facebook use in one year predicted a decrease in mental health in a later year. We found consistently that both liking others' content and clicking links significantly predicted a subsequent reduction in self-reported physical health, mental health, and life satisfaction.

As we can see, striving for happiness isn't always easy and not all relationships are healthy. We should be aiming for meaning and seeking to strengthen real-life connections, not digital ones, rather than fall into the trap Esfahani Smith identifies that if we're not careful, then the search for happiness makes us unhappy.

Article 5—Adopt the New Work Manifesto

CHALLENGE

Workplaces, and work in general, have become bad for us,

really very bad for us. (This isn't an excuse for me to get out of a real job and write books for a living, it's a fact backed up by hard evidence.) Studies show that the length of the average workday has increased by almost 25 percent, a not insignificant creep of a few hours at the beginning and end of the day. The reason? Technology, of course! Our emails and other methods of communication are all pinging to our smartphones, which are by our beds and by our sides at all times. What was once unthinkable (checking messages before getting out of bed, on the toilet, or at family lunch) is now ordinary.

But sadly for us, the increased investment of attention and energy has yielded no positive results, and while the time spent working has increased dramatically, productivity hasn't moved at all. Our overall productivity per hour has dropped. We work more to achieve less, and as a result are more stressed and less able to disconnect from work and reconnect to life. And that's just messages; we haven't even begun to talk about meetings! You're not alone in thinking business meetings as well as emails are by and large a waste of time.

There's an argument that we haven't mastered the energy-saving technology we've invented yet, and that when we do, in a few more years, we'll look back and laugh at (relative to the tools we have) humankind's least productive moment in evolution. I don't know about you, but I'm not thrilled by my long working days being the punch line to some future joke.

But there's more. Multi-tasking: turns out it was a lie. Open-plan offices being good for productivity: also a mistake. Those Microsoft ads that promise we can run a business from the park while playing with our kids, all from a nifty hand-held device: ditto on the bullshit barometer.

For those of you who went to (or attend) university, the way you worked there will be the last time you ever worked sensibly. You agreed on an end goal, you had clear quality measurements and an overall deadline, but then how you worked, the hours you kept, the location, devices, tools, and techniques for getting the work done—they were all up to you. As soon as we "grow up," we graduate into much less sophisticated and sensible metrics, having always to adhere to someone else's time, to be present and concentrate in countless compulsory meetings, and to churn out work to meet standards more to do with timing, budgets, and egos than our own internal measure of quality or satisfaction in a piece of work well done. This means that, quite apart from all that lack of productivity dragging our organizations down, we miss out on the fulfilling reason we humans need to work in the first place.

SUGGESTED ARTICLE

We want to love work, we want to learn as we work, we want to be proud of what we do and have the chance to do it well. We want work to make us better, not worse; we want the rewards of creativity, friendships, fulfillment, and knowledge to match the financial compensation we need. We want life/work balances, not the other way around. We intend to live up to the promise of technology, efficiency, and flexibility. We commit to understanding our own inner engineering for effectiveness and refuse to submit to conditions, clocks, or cultures that don't get the best out of us. We will break the tyranny of emails, meetings, to-do lists, and any other anachronistic trappings of an old way of working, if they don't work for us, and we won't stop until we're judged on our output, not our input.

INSPIRATION

ROW is what you need to know, aka Results Only Work, the brainchild of two workplace productivity consultants Cali Ressler and Jody Thompson who've captured their approach in *Why Work Sucks and How to Fix It: The Results-Only Revolution*.[14] This is a book that everyone who works anywhere needs to read. It explores many ideas that we've looked at and argues that fulfilling our desire for self-direction, autonomy, and accountability leads to greater productivity. In a ROW, you are the boss of your time as long as you deliver the results. Hang the emails, screw the meetings, and forget about turning up on time. It's not actually that radical, but based on the evidence they put forward, it is potentially revolutionary.

The other great mind that's changed my own, and the way I work, and in turn led to the suggestion of this being an essential part of any Pirate Code 2.0, is Cal Newport and his book *Deep Work*.[15] It's Newport who's suggesting our kids will laugh at us from their super-streamlined energy-efficient futures, working only the hours that matter with technology their slave. But he doesn't say it like that, he says it with grace and humor and makes the unquestionably solid case that multitasking, open offices, and in particular notifications are as much good to a productive morning's work as polishing off a few glasses of wine, and a lot less fun. As a direct result of learning from Newport, I stopped responding to emails until midday, which, unless there's an emergency, sounds like a long time, but is a small chunk of the day, and while scary to do, immediately became the most productive and then enjoyable part of it. There's a reason the *Economist* called Newport's book "'The Killer App of the Knowledge

Economy," and it's because it works.

If, unironically, you don't have the time to find out about saving time, that's okay, because a very nice man called Bruce Daisley has created a podcast called Eat Sleep Work Repeat, that, in his own words "helps answer the question 'how can we be happier at work?'" As of the end of 2017, it had topped Tim Ferriss on the iTunes Podcast Top Ten, which, considering Tim Ferriss is a god of professional personal development (and the author of the original 4 Hour Week) and Bruce an unassuming newcomer, says a lot about (a) the appetite for this conversation, (b) the quality of advice and insights on the series, and (c) what a nice chap Bruce is.[16]

The New Work Manifesto is an output of the Eat Sleep Work Repeat series and provides "simple evidence-based ways to improve our jobs" and a clear starting point for anyone interested in not getting lost down a productivity wormhole and embracing some well-founded new ideas about working smarter.[17]

WARNING

It is possible to become obsessed with this topic. Graham Allcott, the excellent author and founder of Productivity Ninja, calls it "Productivity Porn." Basically, there is a whole industry promising to save you time but actually fighting for your attention and selling you apps, books, and conferences. Watch out you don't end up spending more energy on your productivity habit than you save elsewhere.

On the whole, productivity is a lot simpler than you think. It's just about taking a few steps to regain control of your time. When, for so many people, the main culprit for suffocating self-discipline is email, Bruce Daisley in his podcast makes a typically astute observation that while it can seem daunting, when you do push back on technology, and email in particular, it "yields far more easily than you think." So go on, give it a push.

Article 6—Embrace Diversity to Raise Your Game

THE CHALLENGE

"Diversity raises the fucking bar," said Cindy Gallop, the ex–advertising guru and now founder of IfWeRanTheWorld and Make-LoveNotPorn and one of the most creative, outspoken, and brilliant champions of diversity's not just being a box-checking exercise. We know intuitively that diversity matters, but what matters more now is that we make it clear diversity isn't a choice for us to take, it's a change we have to make. By diversity here we're referring to the global conversation that's happening at every level of culture, from the representation of ethnic minorities in Academy Award nominations via the gender pay gap and unbalanced educational achieve-

ment through to unconscious bias in recruitment and cultural misappropriation in the media.

According to the 2017 report "Why Diversity Matters," produced by the consultancy group McKinsey,[18] the evidence is clear: organizations with an ethnically diverse workforce are up to 35 percent more likely to outperform their less diverse rivals, and those that are gender diverse achieve up to 16 percent more than their less diverse competitors. We talk a lot about diversity being the right thing to do, but it's important that the conversation matures to being about the "best" thing to do, for the organization as well as the individual.

Diversity isn't just about good practice, it's about getting to good answers, the ones a complicated world needs. "Everyone in a complex system has a slightly different interpretation. The more interpretations we gather, the easier it becomes to gain a sense of the whole," said Margaret Wheatley, the organizational behaviorist we learned from earlier.[19] It is a cruel irony that in our globalized world, cultural integration is a necessity, yet significant swaths of society are so scared of what that means for their original identity that they violently reject inevitable progress. Margaret acknowledges not just the practical need for diversity but also its power when she says, "You can't hate someone whose story you know."

The conversation is huge, needed, in some instances a little behind the times, and is only going to increase in importance.

But there's a problem. We already risk burnout when the conversation isn't even at a baseline. You see, we're working back from such a deficit, where industry after society after institution remains structurally in favor of middle-class white men, that we're in danger of complacency and mistaking improvement for achievement. At worst, "diversity" is at risk of becoming a trend, a campaign, or even a return to being a box to tick.

SUGGESTED ARTICLE

We believe diversity of thought, background, experience, and understanding is a driver of competitive advantage, creativity, and productive cultures. We who desire to create projects, products, content, and campaigns for the future know the importance of reflecting the future we want to see, one of interconnected, collaborative, communicative, creatively colliding cultures. We commit to recruitment that opens doors to more than the usual suspects, we will go the extra mile to find the talent that might not have found us. We commit to accepting we all have prejudices, and then commit to challenging them, along with expanding our own filter bubbles and stretching our unconscious biases to breaking point.

INSPIRATION

In the early 2000s major institutions around the world welcomed the newest senior hire, the arrival of the chief diversity officer. This was a welcome recognition of the need for a focus on diversity at the highest executive level of any organization and trod the path of chief electricity officers in the early twentieth century and the chief technology officers of the late twentieth century. The trouble is, they all start to feel out-of-date after a time, as the focus they address begins to feel as though it ought to be becoming automatic. The well-intentioned but now anachronistic chief diversity officer is yet another sign that, just as every organization that wanted to survive the Information Age needed a holistic plan for universally embracing digital technology, so too do we need to do our CDOs out of a job. Luckily, there's been an upgrade to the idea, and the best current thinking for anyone in any industry comes from the Great British Diversity Experiment, founded by, among others, Alex Goat, the CEO at Livity.

The first experiment took place in 2016, curating deliberately diverse teams to tackle major industry challenges in order to prove that the breadth of experience within a team increased its chances of finding viable solutions to intractable problems. Safe to say, it was a stunning success. The GBDE's full findings are available to all online.[20] While they're pretty frank, the GBDE are the first to say, "This is not an exercise in industry-bashing but a tool to confront the elephant in the room." And they conclude with several helpful bits of advice for organizations dedicated to creating diverse teams, and three core reasons why diversity makes a positive difference:

1. Being in a diverse working group allows people to be their authentic self—being able to be yourself, and not play to type, means you can contribute

more creatively and be much more effective in your job.

2. It dramatically increases the possibility of new connections between experiences, perspectives, and insights that lead to distinctive, powerful, and new creative ideas.

3. Diversity means ideas develop via meritocracy, and not quick buy-in from the dominant cultural voice. It forces us to be truthful about creative merit rather than fall prey to cultural consensus.

The GBDE is both excellent work in itself and an essential to-do list for any team of any size, but as you work your way through it, there's one last super-simple and accessible trick for your toolkit, and it's called Project Implicit, Harvard University's online implicit bias test.[21] It's a surprise for most people who try it, and usually a useful one, and it's smart enough to update itself regularly, because the really smart people

seeking to overcome their unconscious biases are also using it regularly to measure their progress.

WARNING

The negative effects of a lack of meaningful diversity are self-evident all around the world and across political, social, and economic lines. Understandably, increased division brings greater calls to overcome the diversity gap, a call that often is interpreted as a need for greater empathy—i.e., the ability to understand and share someone else's feelings and experience.

The team at Livity will caution you, because while an admirable ambition, the truth is that making empathy the aim often inadvertently achieves the opposite of increased diversity for the simple reason that human beings are biased and find it much easier to empathize with people who have similar experience sets to their own. We also subconsciously overlook the views of those we don't feel familiar with. As Emily Goldhill, a senior strategist at Livity, puts it, "People's own echo chambers limit their willingness to engage with the unknown. Sometimes they're simply unable to see past their own opinions, which prevents an open dialogue from ever taking place. Empathy, rather than breaking down barriers, can, in fact, reinforce them as support is given to those similar to you, leaving only stony indifference for the rest."[22]

Don't be complacent about the limits of empathy, or our ability to be blind to our own biases. None of us is immune, and the mistakes we make can be costly. Think of the well-intentioned but ultimately fatally flawed Pepsi campaigns starring Kendall Jenner that started out trying to raise a flag for diversity and ended up a joke, to be parodied forevermore.

Create Your Code: Adoption and Adaptation

These proposed articles are assembled from some of the best, bravest, and most badass minds I consider myself lucky to have come across, from all corners of the earth, all sectors, industries, and ages. However, they are all related in that they are from examples of bona fide change-makers, people truly delivering on their promise to make a real difference to their world. They are tried, tested, and trustworthy.

I hope you've seen some articles you'd like to adopt, some you'd like to adapt, some parts of articles that you like, parts you didn't, and probably a whole article or two you disagree with or know is not for you. And that's fine. I've tried to keep the suggested articles within the style of the original codes, and I've tried hard to create ones you might love—but have no sympathy for me: if you hate them, ignore them; write yours and rewrite mine in whatever way that works for you.

The sole aim is to create exciting and inspiring articles that are simple to understand, easy to agree with, and hard to get out of.

So how do you make a code that smells like victory? Creating your Pirate Code is all about adoption and adaptation. Take what you like and change what you don't. You don't have to start from scratch; you don't have to follow anybody else's rules; you can take some and then bend them, or you can steal them with glee exactly as they are. If they work for you, then it's a clear copy-and-paste, open-and-shut case.

While it doesn't matter if your code is an act of piracy, what *is* important is that it's to the point, memorable, short, concise, snappy, accessible, easy, buy-into-able, usable, uncomplicated, and effortless to understand.

You get my drift. It's essential to keep it simple. A good target for any code is between five and ten articles, with each article being a sentence or two at most. Keep your code easy to follow.

But this does not mean codes are easy to create. They require deep thought, and getting to a consensus is almost always tough, even if there's only one of you. Be prepared: it's often harder to get to one clear line that several of you agree on than it is to write a whole page. But this is not like business planning. This is not a process of introspection; this is not supposed to take you away from where you're supposed to be (in front of clients or customers or being creative) for days on end. This is simple and a way of finding your center of gravity before the next adventure starts. You've got to be ready to live or die by them, so get them right. But at the same time, don't panic. New adventure? New crew, new set of articles.

As you prepare to write your own code, please look only for articles that will lift up your heart, your ambitions, your confidence, and your energy levels, so that you will feel good using them to create a fulfilling and successful life. As you consider how to be more pirate in and among the daily grind of your life, make sure you're ready to ride the coming waves, always remembering that you can adapt the code for your next adventure based on what you've learned from the last. Once you've got your code under way, consider how you'll make it memorable.

Way back in the pirate day, each crew member was expected to make their allegiance to the code clear. The more romantic pirate stories tell of sworn oaths over crossed pistols or swords, or an oath taken with hands held upon a human skull or even with a pirate sitting astride a cannon. You can take that as literally as you like, depending on how many swords, skulls, and cannons you have access to, but many successful modern companies test their latest employee's allegiance to their code as soon as they've joined.

Zappos, the wildly successful online retailer (famed for a culture so valuable it led to the company's sale in 2009 for $800 million to Amazon), goes so far as to offer every new starter at the organization $5,000 to leave. It sounds counterintuitive at first, but very quickly and relatively cheaply they distinguish between the starters who intend to stick around and those with a shorter fuse. There are no crossed pistols, but there's also no mistaking that, from that moment forward, you're one of the crew.

What you create as your articles, how you mark the occasion, and how you make your articles memorable is all important, but what's also essential—indeed, the final ingredient necessary to make any code work—is how you make it accountable.

Written in Blood

Creating your code and choosing your crew is one thing, while making it all stick is another. The final piece is how you hold everyone (even if that's only one or two of you) accountable for the choices you make and the code you create.

Authentic accountability is the key to lasting success. Holding yourself and your crew accountable to the articles you agree to is the difference between pirate legend and pirate loser.

The Golden Age pirates, having all signed their codes, ensured an air of authentic accountability hung over them by displaying the code in a prominent place, sometimes over the door of the captain's cabin, sometimes on the mainmast, and always somewhere it could quickly be slung overboard, for it would surely become the pirates' death warrant in the wrong hands. Always too, in the spirit of their total democracy, the articles of association that had been agreed by everyone aboard were also watched over by everyone aboard.

Making your Pirate Code accountable is not an exercise in writing your values on the wall and then forgetting them; this is about writing your own code in your own blood in a way that can never be forgotten.

I don't actually want any of you to write anything in blood—I'm just trying to be dramatic. I want to convey the appropriate sense of importance of the point of pirate accountability, because you really need to focus on this point: the context of accountability and the seriousness with which the code was upheld.

The code was law, and transgressions were unacceptable. It was an act of shared creation and commitment, and it enabled everyone on the crew to look one another in the eye and know they could trust one another with their life to act in honor of the code. Without mutual and binding consent, your code won't hold its full potential or power.

For a shot of rather bracing inspiration that should definitely be taken with a pinch of salt, let's look again to the pirates, specifically one of the articles of Captain John Phillips, which provides an excellent suggestion for motivating consistent behavior:

> If any Man shall steal any Thing in the Company, or
> game, to the Value of a Piece of Eight, he shall be
> marooned or shot.

There's no ambiguity here, no chance of mistake. For the sake of a piece of eight (about $20), there's an almost zero tolerance default to the harshest of punishments. For a bunch of robbers, rascals, and rogues, the regulations were robustly enforced.

These seemingly classic pirate punishments are given more color in William Kidd's code, specifically in this article about embezzlement, ensuring absolutely no thievery among the thieves:

> That if any man shall defraude the company to the value of one piece of eight shall lose his share and be put on shore upon the first inhabited island or other place.

And finally, the code of Bartholomew Roberts contains further developments on robust responsibility and settling disputes onshore:

> If the robbery was only betwixt one another, they contented themselves with slitting the ears and nose of him that was guilty, and set him on shore, not in an uninhabited place, but somewhere, where he was sure to encounter hardships.

Ouch. And not just a marooning, but one with "hardships" and a slit-open bleeding nose and ears. Ouch again.

Just to be clear, neither I nor any of my very nice team at my publishers are suggesting that you actually maroon anyone if they don't follow your code to the letter. But you do need to consider the question of how you maroon them if you need to. Metaphorically speaking.

And to be even clearer, it's not about the threat. I am not advocating threat to get the best out of anyone. Quite the opposite. I've never known a threat to create long-term improvement in performance. It's a dysfunctional way to manage, and blunt threats are rare in the lexicon of real leaders.

Instead, the accountability that is the glue of the Pirate Code is the shared sense of a team signing up to an outcome they all agree is motivating. And while the option of not getting marooned is quite motivating, it's the collective decision-making that really makes this so powerful. It's not rules from the top but a group looking one another in the eye and saying, "If we let each other down, there will be repercussions, and we commit to holding one another to that."

So as you assess your articles, you need to be thinking about these accountability clauses. They can't be pernicious for their own sake, but they do have to be tough, and something that no one on the crew wants to endure.

During the process of writing this book, I've run Pirate Code workshops with entrepreneurs, executives, middle managers, and the most senior leaders. I now gratefully receive messages months after the sessions letting me know their code is "something I use every day" and "one of the most powerful tools I've got at work." But it also means I get to see what people use as their approach to accountability. Here are some I've seen developed that I've been informed worked well:

- Whoever shall break the code buys coffee every morning for everyone else for a week.
- Whoever contravenes this code will be paid a week late.
- Whosoever lets down the crew in the upkeep of this code dress up in any outfit that the crew find suitably amusing and post it to all their social media feeds.
- The one who breaks the code has to take the other one to lunch, anywhere they so choose.

We've all read advice about getting more done, watched a talk about secrets to being more super, and at some point promised ourselves a new habit of improved efficiency or better time management, downloaded a different app, been seduced by the promise of a new pad, or even begun a color coding of our to-do list. Yet here we are again, with a million tabs open, in our minds, screens, and lives, and most of our attention on the stuff that doesn't matter.

The problem is, promises you make to yourself are too easy to break. Making promises to a team makes them more difficult to abandon, which is why the code works, because the promise is made as a group to a group, on simple articles that are easy to sign up to and hard to break.

Which is why this time it will be different. This time you won't be chasing time, you will just be being more pirate. This time you won't have a choice to break your promise, because if you break your Pirate Code, you will be marooned. This time you will create a Pirate Code that you will agree to as a crew, and agree to it one to another, and every member of that crew will have equal say in holding every other member to account.

Now you've got a starting point for your articles, and you've got an accountability or marooning clause in mind, so even if your crew is only you, there is no turning back from the code until the mission is complete, the adventure achieved, and the prize taken.

Choose your code carefully, because the day is yours to win, and it's time to seize it, like a pirate.

It is a true blessing indeed for a man to have a hand determining his own fate.

—Edward Teach, aka Blackbeard

Once again, it's time to pause for processing, to take stock of all that's been presented and digest a little of what's been learned.

In this chapter we've seen some big ideas, some potential parts for you to build your future Pirate Code on, and as such it's time to figure out if all or any of these articles feel right for you.

The articles I included have been designed by others, presented here for you to steal merrily from. They might not ring true or they might have struck a chord. What's important now is picking out the parts that are going to help you change your world.

In workshops I've run, at this point we form participants into small crews to work together to create a series of articles to make their code. I've seen crews break into open mutiny, split, and then re-form with other crews—people tend to take this section very seriously.

And just the same is true for you: this is the momentous occasion when you draft your Pirate Code, establishing you as one of the brethren. It's probably the hardest of all the challenges as you have to pick three, knowing that breaking any of them will leave you "marooned." Because it's the hardest, it is probably also the challenge I've had the most positive feedback from: the forming of a code by a small group has created lasting relationships, has led to dynamic decision-making, and in some instances has totally transformed participants' ways of working for months to come.

So in the space provided, give some thought to the following question:

Which three articles would you be willing to live by?

You do not have to use the ones I've presented to you; you might already have your own or you might admire someone else's out there. It doesn't matter where they come from. For now, just write down three articles that you would use to govern the decision-making of any crew you might have already or might build one day, remembering you have to hold them to account and maroon them if they transgress . . .

I know from experience that this part isn't easy, and if there weren't three or more articles that spoke to you, go to www.bemorepirate.com, where there are more examples.

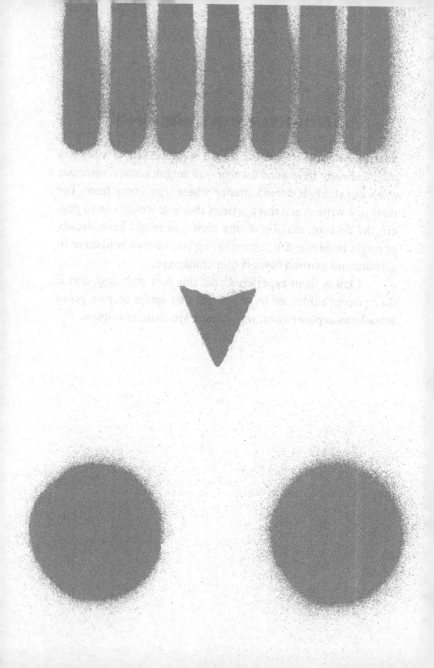

12. THE CALL

Be More You

Here we are almost at the end of the book, and the beginning of your adventure. This is the point where you decide how much more pirate you're going to be. And so far, so pirate, because we've covered a lot. Part One gave us a new understanding and appreciation of pirates as role models as well as rogues. Part Two led us through a five-stage framework that illustrated how you might use the pirates' methods to bring about change. And here, in Part Three, we've uncovered the secret to the pirates' success: their code. You now have your first articles in mind that you'd like to use for the beginnings of your code and be ready to find and create more of your own.

But before you heed the call of your own adventure there are a final few pieces of treasure to share with you. Most important, while we've seen that being more pirate can help you be more dynamic, effective, and influential, it's essential to remember that being more pirate is just a reflection of you, not a replacement for you.

Reflecting on your values, choosing your decision-making principles, and then enshrining them into your own code is how you choose to be more pirate, but it is all also an invitation to be more you, just with a pirate-like sense of confidence, purpose, and mischief.

Pirates were people, too; they were messy, complex, confused, mostly young and trying to make their mark, make some money, and make a better way for themselves. While there is something very special about these pirates that has made their stories endure, there's nothing they did that you can't do. You have the same choice, and chance, as they did. You just need to find your truth, know what future you'd fight for, and after the dust settles, be sure what you treasure.

It's time to choose. Turn pirate and begin your own rebellion, rewrite your own rules, and work through the stages of being more pirate to change your world protected by your Pirate Code . . . or deny your truth and continue to pretend there is no other way than the way things are.

What happens next is up to you. But however you decide to take the tools and techniques of Golden Age pirates into your world, spend as much time making sure you know who you are as you've spent getting to know who these pirates were. Being more pirate can bring out the best in you, but it's up to you to know what your best is.

It's a cliché to say life is short, but the life of a pirate was even shorter, so there is no time to waste. The Pareto principle—used often in economics, although it was originally observed in nature—broadly states that 20 percent of our effort gets us 80 percent of what's worth having. In other words, 80 percent of what you do is largely a waste of time and capacity, spent doing the things that no one, including you, is ever going to remember. A heroic to-do list as long as your arm, a life led by the size of your inbox, being at the mercy of other people's lack of imagination or bad decisions—none of these approaches to getting things done is ever being more pirate.

Knowing what you love, how it feels when you're at your best 20 percent, knowing what you do well, what makes you feel alive, and what you'd die for, and then doing that, and to hell with the 80 percent that is the forgettable rest . . . that is being more pirate.

To take on the world and win, you need to know the few things you think are worth fighting for and ignore the many things worth ignoring. You need to know what you stand for, because otherwise you will fall for anything; you need to know where you're headed and hold on to that, because it's easy to lose your way.

As you think about what type of pirate you'd like to be in this world, I want to offer you one last story from the Golden Age, a cautionary tale of a man who wanted to be more pirate without knowing himself first and who consequently became very lost.

Back we go to the very height of the Golden Age, when everybody knew the pirates' names and everyone wanted some of their game. Summer of 1717, and Stede Bonnet was a well-educated, well-married, and successful plantation owner with no apparent or previous pirate credentials whatsoever. But one day, aged twenty-eight, Bonnet decided to blow the family savings to fund a career change, reinventing himself as "The Gentleman Pirate." He hired a pirate crew, bought a ship, named it *The Revenge*, and left home to turn pirate and go "on the account." Sadly for Stede, he simply wasn't cut out for the pirate life, and in 1718 he was hanged after a year of being possibly the worst pirate ever.

After a few months on the high seas with his own crew, Bonnet was seriously wounded, and soon afterward he ran into Edward Teach, the infamous Blackbeard, who was currently in command of an entire flotilla of pirate ships. Blackbeard took the virginal pirate under his wing and offered to go into "partnership" with him, allowing him to join the growing fleet. As a newbie buccaneer, Bonnet had his work cut out; Blackbeard was just about the toughest act to live up to in all pirate-dom.

The short-lived partnership came to an end once it became clear Bonnet was only a pirate wannabe. Blackbeard began to assume authority over Bonnet's ship and crew and Bonnet's anxiety issues turned into serious depression. As control of his ship slipped from Bonnet, so too did any last pretense of the pirate life; Bonnet took to reading books on deck in his nightwear in the morning. He lost any last vestige of respect he had commanded, and embarrassed by his disregard for keeping up appearances, his crew voted in Blackbeard as their new captain. Bonnet's career as a pirate was all washed up.

Bonnet further cemented his reputation as a person of unpiratical stock at his trial when he blamed his crew for secretly raiding ships as he slept in his bunk, before finally offering to have his own legs and arms chopped off to limit any further piratical misadventures.

Stede Bonnet was hanged at Execution Dock in Charleston, South Carolina, and then his dead body was turned into the most commonly used anti-piracy advertisement of the day as it was suspended above the water for the traditional three tides as warning to any other fool who'd risk their happy home to turn pirate.

In hindsight, Bonnet's desire to adopt John Wayne stances and Errol Flynn advances looks a bit like a midlife crisis. He's that guy who, facing an existential "who am I?" moment, buys a Harley-Davidson he doesn't suit and has a doomed affair. Or in this case an entire pirate ship that didn't suit him and a *very* doomed affair. Bonnet's story is a warning to us all of the need to be able to back up our rebellion, to take small steps and test our ideas, but most of all to be ourselves. If we try to be something we're not and live a lie, then chances are our own inner Blackbeard will lead a mutiny against us and our chance for true adventure will be cut short.

So as you prepare yourself to be more pirate, remember to be more you. Choose the rebellion that speaks to your truth, rewrite the rule that you're excited to share, steal the code that sparks your imagination, live and work by the article that makes you proud. Be more you and you will be more pirate and less Bonnet.

Execute Your Doubts Like the Traitors They Are

In the wake of World War II, legendary anthropologist Margaret Mead spoke at a meeting of great global minds who had come together to discuss nothing less than the future of civilization, where she is believed to have delivered the immortal line: "Never doubt that a small group of thoughtful, committed citizens can change the world; indeed, it is the only thing that ever has." For the last seventy years, small groups of thoughtful citizens and more recently various inspirational Instagram accounts have been quoting this at one another over and over again in the hope that it will come true.

You and I both know it's hard to hold on to the reality of powerful words like these in the cold light of day as the hopes and dreams of so many committed citizens are crushed by the relentless weight of bureaucratic and self-interested systems or just by complacency, laziness, and a lack of imagination.

But even if it's sometimes hard to keep the faith, there is a reason Mead's line is so often quoted: it's because, deep down, we know it's so very true.

Another eminent Margaret, this time Margaret Wheatley, adds to the argument, "All change, even very large and powerful change, begins when a few people start talking with one another about something they care about."[1]

I'm doubling down on the Margarets here because I am hoping so hard that you can hang on to this deceptively straightforward but powerful point that both underlines all we've learned about pirates and informs all the power you can achieve by being more pirate.

You've inherited a system so broken that anything less than a radical alternative is suicidal; we're trying to grow in an economy and ecosystem that can barely support the size we are; we're run by an establishment willing to sell out the biosphere to improve a budget line; and above it all, we accept a global "wisdom" that dictates this way is the only way to keep living. The future holds an almost guaranteed major cataclysmic event in your lifetime, where the only certain truth will be that no one is coming to save you.

But accepting this reality need not be intimidating or overwhelming—it is just a fact of your future. We're not here to write the global policy to save the world. We are here to work out what good trouble we can cause at the edges, as small groups of pirates; what ideas we can share that will create waves to cause an effect on the middle. To achieve this act of pirate influence, we are the only leaders we need; we must just take that step of rebellion, followed by some rule rewriting, to start to assemble some small crews with a Pirate Code that's tough enough to help them ride the storm.

It's important to admit that doing something new, challenging something old, or creating almost any degree of change can feel uncomfortable, scary, and hard for most of us. Whether you're on your own or have a brilliant crew around you, change creates a degree of anxiety in most people, most of the time. We've been so hardwired to avoid discomfort, mess, and chaos that it's easy to get discouraged at the first hurdle or when everything doesn't fall into place as quickly as you expect it to. But we need to learn to embrace this feeling. If pursuing your idea makes you at least a little bit anxious, then you're probably doing something right, and anything less is probably complacency. It's almost impossible to break something or try to build something without running into problems and a little awkwardness. Like pirates, we need to get comfortable feeling uncomfortable. We need to make friends with mess and get cozy with a little chaos and accept that these are helpful and positive first parts of the process of creating change.

Compound Imagination

When you begin your journey to pirate-inspired change, it doesn't matter if you don't know what the end game looks like; all that matters is that you make a start. Far too many of us don't ever make that first step because we get obsessed with worrying about what the final outcome will or won't be, or worrying about what's beyond our control; this is a surefire step to being less pirate.

In fact, not knowing what's in the final chapter when you start writing the book means you'll be in good company. Not knowing what's off the edge of the map is what made the pirates successful. Not knowing the compounding potential of where your own ideas might end up is a fine place to start. As long as you start, anyway.

Did the Lumière brothers create cinema only to miss the whole point of popcorn, date nights, blockbusters, kissing in the dark, art house, and everything else that's amazing about the movies and to declare their invention had "no future"? Yup.

Did Alexander Graham Bell invent the telephone only to find he preferred the written telegram and therefore to dismiss what would become the defining piece of technology of the twenty-first century as only a "toy"? He sure did.

Did Thomas Edison produce the phonograph but fail to see the pleasure (or the phenomenal commercial opportunity) of playing music at home, believing that the machine he'd created was like a massive Dictaphone for businessmen only? You betcha.

Did Ada Lovelace, as she wrote the first algorithmic program to be carried out by a computer, consider the profound relationship between individuals and society and how they might relate to technology as a collaborative tool? Well, actually she did, but then maybe she's just a stroke smarter than the other chaps.

But chiefly, did the pirates set out to predate many of modern civilization's most socially progressive advances when they wrote their Pirate Codes?

Of. Course. Not. They were just trying to organize themselves better than they had been in the navy, and without the abuse. But, you see where I'm coming from.

With the benefit of historical hindsight, it can seem ridiculous that these rebels weren't aware of the full potential of their ideas when they were rewriting the conventions of their time. So rather than be daunted or dissuaded by the scale of the challenge, instead derive pleasure from taking small but well-intentioned steps.

Malala started with a blog. RZA started with a $300 recording session. Steve Jobs started hacking free phone calls at a nerds' computer club. Chance the Rapper started with an online mixtape. I started with a rave in a Kwik Save car park.

Take inspiration from these rebels and start with small, strategic pirate moves, designed to hit where it hurts. A swift kick in even the biggest balls can topple almost any enemy. And a small idea can turn into something momentous when its hour comes. The more you take care developing your idea, experimenting with it, testing it, and sharing it, the stronger it becomes.

When I talk about ideas compounding, I've taken

inspiration from and stolen the law of compound interest and named it "compound imagination," because I believe the same laws apply. Albert Einstein reportedly said that compound interest is the eighth wonder of the world, and before him Benjamin Franklin certainly knew the power of it, too. When he died in 1790 he left his two favorite cities, Boston and Philadelphia, $5,000 each in a compound account, with a strict covenant that the cities weren't allowed to touch it until 1991, when both received $20 million.

The principle underlying compounding is powerful, and I've raised it here because it is written into and across the five stages of pirate change—one small act of rebellion becomes a mutiny, and that mutiny proposes a better rule and way of doing things that is experimented with, tweaked through collaboration, and scales to a point where it influences the mainstream. By taking a small idea and developing it, testing it, growing it, this is how a small group of committed citizens can change the world. And the Pirate Code is the insurance to protect your investment.

C. S. Lewis pointed out that both "Good and evil increase at compound interest. That's why the little decisions we make every day are of infinite importance."[2] The author concludes, "the smallest good act today is the capture of a strategic point from which, a few months later, you may be able to go on to victories you never dreamed of."

This is why it doesn't matter if your crew is big or small. This is why it doesn't matter if your idea is fully formed or in its earliest incarnation. This is why intention is everything and small crews are the perfect way to get started. These are the reasons why the pirates' ideas went from a tiny corner of the Caribbean to making the whole world shake. Whether you're going up against injustice or you want to change something in your street, job, class, or community, start like a pirate and see where it will take you.

Anne Bonny ran away to sea and ended up the inspiration for the Lady of Liberty. Henry Morgan started on a humble farm in Wales, yet he defined an age, became a legend, and inspired a different and dynamic organizational system. "Black" Sam Bellamy was born the youngest of six and ran away to sea as a boy, yet he became the Prince of Pirates, the articulate incarnation of their most progressive ideals of fairness, justice, and equality that at the time sounded like outright rebellion, and now sound like a lesson for all of us.

All that really matters now is that you begin.

Just as Morgan, Bellamy, and Bonny once did, you look out to an uncertain horizon of opportunity, unfairness, chance, and change, now armed with the tactics and techniques to be more pirate to help you find success. If you take only one thing from all we've tried to cover, please let it be this: what happens next is up to you.

PIRATES *Draw Strength from Standing Up to the Status Quo*

PIRATES *Bend, Break, and Ultimately Rewrite the Rules*

PIRATES *Collaborate to Achieve Scale Rather Than Growth*

PIRATES *Fight for Fairness and Make Enemies of Exploitation*

PIRATES *Weaponize Stories, Then Tell the Hell Out of Them*

Pirates Assemble

Twelve months ago, I thought I was writing a book about a metaphor for doing things differently, but as I am finishing it, I realize that it was a lot more than a metaphor; and is now much more than a book. *Be More Pirate* is now a talk and a workshop. *Be More Pirate* is a project and a platform. *Be More Pirate* is a conversation and a community.

Whether I've been delivering the talk in Africa, Europe, or America, it's become clear that many people share the same fears about the future of our world and feel passionately about our role in creating a new system for change. They are looking for a new way to think, work, and live. They are calling for change. They are looking for new role models, new modes of organizing, and new ways to work.

If you've felt the call, then join us at www.bemorepirate .com, where a small group of thoughtful and committed pirates are sharing ideas about how to cause good trouble, how to take on the world and win, and how to be more pirate.

Come and join the rebellion.

13. THE PIRATE LIST

Sometimes it's tough to be more pirate when you're lost in a spreadsheet, dying inside as you open another PowerPoint slide, or watching your card get declined because you just quit your job for that world-changing dream, or because you're actually doing the start-up thing and are learning the harsh reality that the hustle ain't easy. There will be moments, days even, where you don't think you can be more pirate. On days like these you need to dig down and find courage and look to other pirates for inspiration.

There are plenty of brilliant individuals, groups, organizations, and communities who are already pirate-like in nature, operating on the edges of industries, seeking new ideas, and inspiring new generations. Over the course of my career and the writing of this book I've come across thousands of pioneers who are trying to break rules and make better ones, who don't seem scared to be different, and are trying to reorganize their worlds for the better.

I've taken the liberty of listing a few of my favorites, from Patreon to Taylor Swift. Hopefully they aren't all obvious, but they all are using the pirate stages of change, and they are all operating by some kind of code of their own.

Use this list as you like. Check out one, check out none, or check out all of them. They are here to excite and motivate you to be more pirate, just when you think you can't.

Quite deliberately in no particular order, and by no means intended to be exhaustive, here are seventeen pirates to inspire you. For more, go to www.bemorepirate.com.

1. **ESCAPE THE CITY** got wise to the fact that smart people are starting to demand more than money from their jobs long before the global reports told us that people want to work in a place that has a purpose, and that we all work better when our work has a meaning. Escape the City started out as a newsletter of opportunities for bored city workers to apply their professional talents in paid roles but for organizations that made the world a better place. They soon became a reverse recruitment agency, saving great talent from being wasted in the financial sector and channeling it in service of a greater good.

2. **PROFESSOR MUHAMMAD YUNUS** came up with the world-changing idea of microfinance when he decided to lend rather than give money to a woman he saw begging in the same place every day. On the back of such a big but simple idea he built Grameen, a super network of social businesses from fisheries to telecoms that lifted millions from poverty by giving them a fairer deal. On a mission to "put poverty in a museum," Yunus has landed in serious trouble with his own Bangladeshi government for his fearlessness and frankness, but has also won a Nobel Prize for Peace and created social business partnerships with brands from Danone to Adidas.

3. **SOPHI TRANCHELL** is in a league of her own. She founded Divine Chocolate back when a Fairtrade logo on food meant it cost more and tasted worse than its unfair alternatives. Sophi played the multitrillion-dollar chocolate industry at its own game and won. Not only did Sophi create an enviable brand that demanded shelf space in high-end retailers, she also conquered the fierce battleground of supermarket chains, all while ensuring that Ghanaian chocolate farmers owned and comanaged the company through a high degree of transparency and shared governance. Sophi's success led directly to the chocolate-producing multinationals adopting Fairtrade suppliers; the navy took from the pirate.

4. **SATOSHI NAKAMOTO** in true pirate style remains anonymous; no one really knows the true identity of the inventor of the world's first cryptocurrency, and let's be honest, no one really knows how it works either. But it does, and since its release in 2009 Bitcoin has had the world's financial markets trembling in awe of a "decentralized currency." With rules they don't understand, with no country to whom it belongs, with only the citizens of the internet as its users, and with stock market valuations accelerating, it is set to create huge waves.

5. **PAM WARHURST** started a revolution using food to change the way people live and learn when she launched Incredible Edible in a small market town in the north of England. On spare land, in people's

gardens, and even in front of the police station, Pam and her crew planted "propaganda gardening" that changed a community's relationship with food, nature, and eventually itself. Pam and her vegetable pirates became an internet sensation and sparked a global movement when Pam's TED Talk inspired hundreds of communities to reclaim unused land and use it to educate, feed, and inspire. There are now over 100 Incredible Edible groups in the UK and many more that span the world, radically repurposing land to grow vegetables in order to rebalance communities and their relationship with nature.

6. **PATREON** is a revolution for the individuals and organizations in the creative economy, for the first time enabling artists, makers, and creators effectively to allow their audience to subscribe to their work, and pay nominal amounts in real time as they produce, rather than have to finance entire projects and productions themselves. It's fast becoming one of the most important creative networks in the world; launched in 2013, within five years it had grown to a body of over 50,000 creatives collectively receiving $150 million in regular small installments from a global audience of millions.

7. **JAMAL EDWARDS** was a teenager who started filming East London's MCs from the grime scene. Seeking exclusive snippets of content and freestyle raps, he filmed at night,

edited until morning, uploaded to YouTube, and saw his following grow and grow until his platform became the number one site for any artist coming to the UK. Jamal eventually found himself on tour with Jay Z, appointed as the face of Google's TV campaign, pictured on billboards, and honored by the queen. All the time using his story and influence to create even bigger waves, Jamal inspired thousands of other young people to follow in his footsteps.

8. **GIRL EFFECT** was a simple idea with huge potential that, in the hands of some of the world's greatest storytellers, rewrote the rule book of international development. The Girl Effect argues that investing in girls in developing countries creates the greatest possible multiple of a return because it (a) sidesteps the common dangers of corruption, (b) is a genuine investment in the future, and (c) empowers a group more usually overlooked and undervalued. Behind its success is the Nike Foundation, whose budgets and branding skills have allowed Girl Effect to disrupt the way traditional aid is being delivered.

9. **TAYLOR SWIFT** might seem to be an unlikely-looking buccaneer, but she is a pirate through and through. Rejecting the obvious record-industry route, Taylor is signed to a small-town label where she retains complete control of her career. With no industry machine to back

her, she's nevertheless amassed the clout to stand up to Apple and Spotify and bring them both to heel. Her storytelling through song, content, social media, and well-orchestrated gossip, vendettas, and "feuds" with everyone from Kanye West to Katy Perry means she's routinely named on social media among the world's most powerful figures.

10. **MEXICO CITY** is one of the largest and oldest cities in the world. Beset by corruption and narco traffic, it is not the obvious center of civic innovation, yet by defying immense odds, standing up to its challenges, and breaking all the rules of a very traditionally Catholic country, it is doing exactly that. Mexico City has engaged in one of the largest exercises in participatory democracy in the world, with citizens helping shape policy online, leading to breakthrough innovations in social policy from abortion on request to a limited form of legal euthanasia to no-fault divorce to same-sex marriage. It is also actively encouraging social enterprise communities, effecting transformation in education, and taking a firm stance against corruption.

11. **RESPONSIVE.ORG** is a whole new way of organizing. It's a manifesto for change that could affect every organization in the world, from Microsoft to Pepsi, to governments, charities, start-ups, and multinationals. Responsive has published a manifesto for the next it-

eration of organizational theory, which they believe is going to be "self-organizing." They advocate being "built to learn" with rapid response mechanisms designed into how teams operate and process information and create work. They encourage experimentation and continuous improvement, and argue it's achievable if we move to a new paradigm where employees and customers exist within the same network all aligned around a shared purpose. There might not be as many buzzwords in the future, but there will definitely be Responsive organizations.

12. **MEU RIO** is an awesome force giving real strength to the collective voice of Rio de Janeiro's youth. With thousands and thousands of young people signed up, it's a platform politicians can't ignore, and since its launch in 2011 it has had some considerable wins, adding further to its reputation as a powerful network of youth. Blocking corrupt politicians, protecting a school from closure, and preserving environmental policies in the city are among its triumphs so far. But its most considerable achievement is proving that an organized, collaborative, participatory group of young people can change their world.

13. **EDWARD SNOWDEN** put more than his career on the line, risking a court-martial and a long prison sentence when he turned whistle-blower on the Central Intelligence Agency (CIA) and the National Security Agency (NSA)

of the United States of America (USA), telling the world that these organizations have got us all under surveillance—a fact they'd rather keep secret.

14. **WIKILEAKS** might have a founder more famous for allegations against his behavior, but the work of the organization is what gets it a place on the list. Having become the go-to platform for sharing the truth when it's too hot to handle, WikiLeaks has become a conduit between the whistle-blowers the world needs to keep it accountable and the media whose job that's supposed to be.

15. **MATT STONE AND TREY PARKER** broke and rewrote the rules with *South Park*, their anarcho-cartoon that broke the accepted boundaries of what was considered appropriate to laugh at. Their searing satire has everything in its sights from Jesus (regularly) to gender politics, cultural identities, politicians, big business, and capitalism. There are few important aspects of society they haven't somehow widened the lens on by making incredibly funny, incredibly crass jokes about them.

16. **DEVELOPMENT MONITOR** takes one of the toughest truths going and turns it into accessible data anyone in the world can use. All their robust and transparently collected evidence suggests the commonly held perception that international aid is beneficial to developing countries may well be based on bad math. They calculate and demonstrate that due to the bigger

mechanisms of market forces, for every $1 put into a "developing country" by another government's charity or international development budget, usually the equivalent of $2 is extracted. There have been many calls for an improvement on the effectiveness of well-intentioned international development to innovate beyond any accusations of evolved colonialism. But it's Development Monitor who are making the argument unignorable.

17. **THE *GUARDIAN* NEWSPAPER** was born with real pirate roots, when its founder, John Edward Taylor, read in *The Times* a biased report of workers' riots he'd witnessed firsthand. The idea for an impartial investigative newspaper came to him. Ever since, *The Guardian* has fought for those principles, its independence guaranteed by well-invested and well-protected financial reserves held in trust. The newspaper has acquired a global reputation for brave journalism and taken on anyone who gets in the way of telling an important story; many of the major game-changing news stories of the last few years have *Guardian* journalists behind them, from the Panama and the Paradise Papers through to the infamous phone-hacking scandal across the Murdoch-owned media. In keeping with its journalistic ideals, the paper remains innovative in its business model, exploring ways to generate income that protect its independence and integrity. In 2017 it both launched an enterprise

accelerator investing financially in new innovations, and garnered a record number of paying subscribers, with 800,000 readers around the world pledging to support the *Guardian*'s journalistic principles and approach.

You'll find more examples of pirate-like pioneers and inspiring ideas on www.bemorepirate.com.

Now and then we had a hope that if we lived and were good, God would permit us to be pirates.

—Mark Twain

ACKNOWLEDGMENTS

Thank you.

Firstly, to my beautiful and brilliant wife, for the patience, love, and support it takes to put up with a grown man, husband, and father who wants so much to be a pirate: thank you and I love you.

Then there are lots of pirate crews I would like to thank for the adventures that enabled me to arrive at *Be More Pirate*, several of whom I've fought alongside in too many adventures to mention, but all of whom have provided inspiration during my ongoing journey of exploration in how to take on the world and win, especially the many thousands of young people who've made my work something worth living for. All the Livity old school: Michelle Morgan, Kate Brundle, Callum Mc-Geogh, Lianre Robinson, Lyeloon Kazi, Paola Dos Santos, Mark Gurney, Jo McCarthy, Josh Connell, Oyin Akini, Mira Jesani, Maya Debowska, Charlotte Livingstone, Aisha Siddiq, Jamie Scoular, Will De-Groot, Torri Stewart, Josh Denton, Natasha Hanckell-Spice, and so many more. And massive respect to the Livity new school, and future: Katy Woodrow Hill, Tom Ellis, James Hogwood, Ty Stanton, Gillian Jackson, Flossy Harwood, Stacey Stollery, Felix Morgan, Aishat Ola-Said, Hannah Owens, Alice McDonnell, Suzi Bielski, Shahnaz Ahmed, James Honess, Karina Tcakzyk, Stephen Woodford, Lucy Inmonger, Raf Gooverts, and of course the Boss, Alex Goat. There are hundreds of

Livity pirates in between who are too numerous to mention, but I thank you sincerely for all the world-changing adventures. All the Livity Africa Team, especially Gavin Weale, Tarin Ayres, Siphiwe Mpye, Karein Bezuidenhout, Nkuli Mlangeni, and Ditiro Madiseng. A massive thank-you for fifteen years of team *Live* magazine: Jordan Jarrett-Bryan, Cleo Soazandry, Aziza Francis, Sian Anderson, Frances Acquaah, Sonia Teibowei, Shola Aleje, Dan Brigante, Kalise Cross, Zezi Ifore, Jelani DeCosta, Henry Houdini, Dan Dutt-Hemp, Patrick Columbus, Mario Arimana, Mann Ray Powell, Tony Mitsinga, Shanize Henry, Bejay Munega, Christina Lai, Robbie Wojciechowski, Terri Brown, Celeste Houlke, Bianca Gill, Eve-Yasmin, Andrea Garisom, Emma Warren, Rahul Verma, Chantelle Fiddy, Kay Dalami, and *so* many thousands more. An enormous thank-you to team somewhereto_ including Tom Barratt, Joe Gray, Shady Bajelvand, #Dwain Lucktung, Jiselle Steele, Anna Hamilos, Athena Simpson, Jason Page, Tina Barton, Esther Brown, Terence Wallen, Yelena Kleyner, and again so many more. Mr. Joe Wade of Don't Panic. The Dubplate Pioneers, Luke Hyams, Louis Figgis, and Justin Stennet. Surash Kara, my partner in DocuMovie. The Social Enterprise Ambassadors. The whole Amaphiko family, but particularly Raluca Simiuc and Uncle Ian Calvert. Team UnDivided, especially Elspeth Hoskins, Joe Porter, Elliot Goat, Charlotte Gerada, Hafsah Dabiri, Rob Wilson, David Reed, Jamie Mccoll, Edward Boott, and all thousands of young people involved. Dan, Rob, Luke, and all the Foundrs pirates. To my mentors, Liam Black, Max Alexander, and Sinclair Beecham, without whom I'd have fallen off the map many more times. And to all the rest of you from so many projects, plans, dreams, and schemes who were part of the good fight, part of the Livity family, or part of any of my many adventures over the last twenty years trying to do something that means something, thank you.

Thanks also to the crew at Penguin Random House who have proven themselves fine pirates, especially Lydia Yadi and David Over, first among Penguin pirates, but also Fred Baty, Joel Rickett, John Hamilton, Chris Bentham, Richard Bravery, Mathias Lord, Celia Buzuk, Joanna Prior, Tom Weldon as well as Helen Coyle and Trevor Horwood. Thanks to my Simon & Schuster editor, Matthew Benjamin.

Thanks especially to the brethren whose contributions have regularly been the wind in my sails in making this adventure happen: Jon Alexander, whose ideas of citizenship underpin this book. Rod Stanley, for introducing me to good trouble. Callum McGeogh, for the inspiration, as ever. Emma Warren and Florence Wilkinson, for being my first critics. Jill from the *Phoenix* and now the *Express* for the sustenance and early morning place to write. And a host of inspirations, conversations, critics, expertise, and inspiration on all fronts from covers to content: Oli Barrett, Andy Last, Jonathan Wise, Shahnaz Ahmed, Gabbi Cahane, Michal Bohanes, Tim Smale, Joe Wade, Charlotte Day-Lewin, Lauren Grant, Vinny Maddage, Adrian Valencia, Luke Hyams, Bryn Walbrook, Pascal Meline, Sara Bender, Justine Clement, Sara Milne-Rowe, Gillian Lonergan, Sherilyn Shackell, Natasha Merrington, Daniel Solomons, Saul Parker, Andrew Bloch, Thyme Mor, Harry Harrison, Joe Kibria, and most of all, Adam Day-Lewin for your continuous creative contribution, encouragement, enthusiasm, bad jokes, and support.

A very significant thank-you to all the academics, historians, economists, authors, and enthusiasts on whose work I relied so heavily and to whom I apologize for my lack of academic rigor and historical training; I hope I've done your work some justice: Marcus Rediker, Peter Earle, David Cordingly, Peter Leeson, Rodolphe Durand and Jean-Philippe Vergne, E. T. Fox, Douglas Burgess, Benerson Little, Alexa Clay, Mayra Phillips, Matt Mason, Adam Morgan, Angus Konstam, Kester Brewin, Laura Sook Duncombe, Philip Gosse, Kester Brewin, Frederic Laloux, Margaret Wheatley, Daniel Defoe, and of course Captain Johnson, but above all Matt Albers at the Pirate History Podcast for being the soundtrack to my writing. And, if anyone can help me find him, I'd like to thank Peter Hicks, my secondary-school history teacher, who probably has no idea the inspiration he had on me. Last, and by no means least, a final thank-you to my mum and dads, because what thank-you would be complete without that, just as I would not be complete without them.

NOTES

1. Here Be Dragons

1. Guy Anthony De Marco, "Foreword" to Philip Gosse, *The Pirate Who's Who*, expanded ed., Warped Mind Press, 2015, p. 1.

2. Jon Ronson, *The Psychopath Test: A Journey Through the Madness Industry*, Picador, 2011.

3. Peter Leeson, *The Invisible Hook: The Hidden Economics of Pirates*, Princeton University Press, 2011, p. 101.

4. Nirad Chaudhuri, "Reflections on the Organizing Principle of Pre-modern Trade," in James D. Tracy, ed., *The Political Economy of Merchant Empires: State Power and World Trade, 1350–1750*, Cambridge University Press, 1993, pp. 421–42.

5. Peter Linebaugh and Marcus Rediker, *The Many-Headed Hydra: Sailors, Slaves, Commoners, and the Hidden History of the Revolutionary Atlantic*, repr. ed., Beacon Press, 2013, p. 168.

6. https://piratehistorypodcast.com, Episode 1.

2. Enemies of Humanity

1. Paul Hodgson, "Top CEOs Make More Than 300 Times the Average Worker" *Fortune*, June 22, 2015, http://fortune.com/2015/06/22/ceo-vs-worker-pay/.

2. Rodolphe Durand and Jean-Philippe Vergne, *The Pirate Organization: Lessons from the Fringes of Capitalism*, Harvard Business Review Press, 2012, p. 162.

3. "Elon Musk's Mission to Mars," *Wired*, October 21, 2012, www.wired .com/2012/10/ff-elon-musk-qa/.

4. Daniel Chaitin, "John Lewis Encourages 'Necessary Trouble' Against Injustice in America," *Washington Examiner*, May 13, 2017, www.washing tonexaminer.com/john-lewis-encourages-necessary-trouble-against-injus tice-in-america/article/2623032.

4. Rebels with a Cause

1. Marcus Rediker, *Villains of All Nations: Atlantic Pirates in the Golden Age*, Verso, 2004, p. 174.

2. Kester Brewin, *Mutiny! Why We Love Pirates, and How They Can Save Us*, Vaux, 2016.

3. Margaret J. Wheatley, *Turning to One Another: Simple Conversations to Restore Hope to the Future*, Berrett-Koehler, 2002.

4. Captain Charles Johnson, *A General History of the Robberies and Murders of the Most Notorious Pyrates*, 1724; repr., Routledge, 2002, p. 482.

5. Anonymous, *Radio Is My Bomb: A DIY Manual for Pirates*, Hooligan Press, 1987.

6. Matt Mason, *The Pirate's Dilemma: How Youth Culture Is Reinventing Capitalism*, Free Press, 2008.

7. Lawrence Lessig, *Free Culture: The Nature and Future of Creativity*, published online under the Creative Commons Attribution/Non-commercial license on March 25, 2004.

5. Rewrite Your Rules

1. https://en.wikipedia.org/wiki/Mutiny.

2. See www.pretotyping.org/.

3. Daniel Defoe and Captain Charles Johnson, *A General History of the Pyrates*, 1724; repr., CreateSpace, 2014, p. 73.

4. Captain Charles Johnson, *A General History of the Robberies and Murders of the Most Notorious Pyrates*, 1724; repr., Routledge, 2002, p. 126.

5. Marcus Rediker, "Liberty Beneath the Jolly Roger," in Margaret S. Creighton and Lisa Norling, eds., *Iron Men and Wooden Women: Gender and Seafaring in the Atlantic World, 1700–1920*, Johns Hopkins University Press, 1996, pp. 1–33, p. 8.

6. Ibid., p. 15.

7. Ibid., p. 11.

8. Ibid., p. 18.

9. Ibid., p. 22.

10. Elon Musk, "Essay in Aeon," 2016, https://aeon.co/essays/elon-musk-puts-his-case-for-a-multi-planet-civilisation.

11. "Why Chance the Rapper Is Forgoing Solo Fame to Make Jazzy Songs with Friends," www.thefader.com/2015/01/29/chance-the-rapper-donnie-trumpet-the-social-experiment-cover-story.

12. "Chance the Rapper on Staying Independent: 'It's a Dead Industry,'" www.rollingstone.com/music/news/chance-the-rapper-on-staying-independent-its-a-dead-industry-20130927.

6. Reorganize Yourself

1. Frederic Laloux, *Reinventing Organizations*, Nelson Parker, 2014, p. 29.

2. Olivia Solon, "The Year That Silicon Valley Lost Its Grip on Reality," *Guardian*, December 24, 2017, www.theguardian.com/technology/2017/dec/22/tech-year-in-review-2017.

3. Margaret Wheatley and Deborah Frieze, "Lifecycle of Emergence: Using Emergence to Take Social Innovation to Scale," *Kosmos*, 14, no. 2 (Spring–Summer 2014), p. 45, http://margaretwheatley.com/wp-content/uploads/2014/12/KosmosJournal-WheatleyFrieze-SS15.pdf.

4. www.fahrenheit-212.com/boiling-point/the-paradox-of-scale.

5. Kenneth J. Kinkor, "Black Men Under the Black Flag," in C. R. Pennell, ed., *Bandits at Sea: A Pirates Reader*, New York University Press, 2001, pp. 194–210, p. 201.

6. Ibid.

7. Marcus Rediker, "The Seaman as Pirate: Plunder and Social Banditry at Sea," in C. R. Pennell, ed., *Bandits at Sea: A Pirates Reader*, pp. 139–68, p. 144.

8. https://index.okfn.org/place/.

9. https://platform.coop/about.

10. Ibid.

11. "Avaaz Faces Questions Over Role at Centre of Syrian Protest Movement," *Guardian*, March 2, 2012.

12. https://www.avaaz.org/page/en/about/.

7. Redistribute Power

1. Peter Leeson, *The Invisible Hook: The Hidden Economics of Pirates*, Princeton University Press, 2011, p. 69.

2. Ibid., p. 24.

3. "Millennials Ditching Graduate Jobs at Big Firms in Favour of Founding Startups, Research Suggests," www.independent.co.uk/news/business/news/millennials-ditching-graduate-jobs-at-big-firms-in-favour-of-founding-startups-research-suggests-a7999231.html.

4. "Aspirational Consumers Are Rising. Are Brands Ready to Meet Them?", https://globescan.com/aspirational-consumers-are-rising-are-brands-ready-to-meet-them/.

5. "The 2015 Deloitte Millennial Survey," www2.deloitte.com/al/en/pages/human-capital/articles/2015-deloitte-millennial-survey.html.

8. Retell Tall Tales

1. Angus Konstam, *Blackbeard: America's Most Notorious Pirate*, Wiley, 2006, p. 293.

2. Daniel Defoe and Captain Charles Johnson, *A General History of the Pyrates*, 1724; repr., CreateSpace, 2014, pp. 37–38.

3. Philip Gosse, *The Pirate Who's Who*, expanded ed., Warped Mind Press, 2015, p. 313.

4. Colin Woodard, "The Last Days of Blackbeard," *Smithsonian*, February 2014, www.smithsonianmag.com/history/last-days-blackbeard-180949440 /?all%205.

5. Douglas R. Burgess, Jr., *The Pirates' Pact: The Secret Alliances Between History's Most Notorious Buccaneers and Colonial America*, McGraw-Hill, 2008.

6. Gosse, *The Pirate Who's Who*, p. 40.

7. Burgess, *The Pirates' Pact*, p. 240.

8. Matt Albers, personal communication.

9. Burgess, *The Pirates' Pact*, p. 265.

10. "The Audacity of Talking About Race with the Ku Klux Klan," *Atlantic*, March 2015, www.theatlantic.com/politics/archive/2015/03 /the-audacity-of-talking-about-race-with-the-klu-klux-klan/388733/.

11. Ibid.

12. Peter Beaumont, "Palestinians Crash Banksy 'Street Party' Satirising Balfour Celebrations," *Guardian*, November 1, 2017, www.theguardian .com/world/2017/nov/01/palestinians-crash-banksy-street-party-seeking -apology-for-balfour-declaration.

13. Banksy, *Banging Your Head Against a Brick Wall*, Banksy, 2001.

10. Original Pirate Material

1. Kenneth J. Kinkor, "Black Men Under the Black Flag," in C. R. Pennell, ed., *Bandits at Sea: A Pirates Reader*, New York University Press, 2001, pp. 194–210, p. 201.

2. Arne Bialuschewski, "Black People Under the Black Flag: Piracy and the Slave Trade on the West Coast of Africa, 1718–1723," *Slavery and Abolition* 29 (December 2008), pp. 461–75, https://doi.org/10.1080/01440390802486473.

3. Edward Theophilus Fox, "'Piratical Schemes and Contracts': Pirate Articles and Their Society, 1660–1730," submitted to the University of Exeter as a thesis for the degree of doctor of philosophy in maritime history, May 2013.

4. Ibid.

5. Ibid.

6. The UN Secretary-General's Report on Cooperatives in Social Development (A/70/61) of 2015, www.un.org/development/desa/cooperatives/2016/02/29/cooperative-newsletter-january-2016/.

11. The Pirate Code 2.0

1. Simon Sinek, *Start with Why: How Great Leaders Inspire Everyone to Take Action*, Penguin, 2011, www.ted.com/talks/simon_sinek_how_great_leaders_inspire_action.

2. Jon Alexander, "Sensemaking / The Consumer Is Dead! Long Live the Citizen," https://thefuturescentre.org/articles/8240/opinion-consumer-dead-long-live-citizen.

3. www.citizenshift.info/.

4. www2.deloitte.com/uk/en/pages/technology-media-and-telecommunications/articles/mobile-consumer-survey.html.

5. www.hsph.harvard.edu/news/features/advertisings-toxic-effect-on-eating-and-body-image/.

6. www.sheffield.ac.uk/news/nr/social-media-economics-research-happiness-1.694959.

7. Simon Leigh and Steve Flatt, "App-Based Psychological Interventions: Friend or Foe?", *Evidence Based Mental Health* 18, no. 4 (November 2015), http://ebmh.bmj.com/content/18/4/97.

8. "New Study Shows We Work Harder When We Are Happy," Warwick University press release, March 2014, https://warwick.ac.uk/newsand events/pressreleases/new_study_shows/.

9. Paul Dolan, *Happiness by Design*, Avery, 2014.

10. www.edx.org/course/science-happiness-uc-berkeleyx-gg101x-6.

11. www.ted.com/talks/emily_esfahani_smith_there_s_more_to _life_than_being_happy.

12. www.adultdevelopmentstudy.org/.

13. Holly B. Shakya and Nicholas A. Christakis, "A New, More Rigorous Study Confirms: The More You Use Facebook, the Worse You Feel," *Harvard Business Review*, April 10, 2017, https://hbr.org/2017/04/a-new -more-rigorous-study-confirms-the-more-you-use-facebook-the-worse -you-feel.

14. Cali Ressler and Jody Thompson, *Why Work Sucks and How to Fix It: The Results-Only Revolution*, Penguin, 2008.

15. Cal Newport, *Deep Work: Rules for Focused Success in a Distracted World*, Piatkus, 2016.

16. Bruce Daisley, Eat Sleep Work Repeat, https://itunes.apple.com /gb/podcast/eat-sleep-work-repeat/id1190000968?mt=2.

17. https://newworkmanifesto.org/.

18. Vivian Hunt, Dennis Layton, and Sara Prince, "Why Diversity Matters," www.mckinsey.com/business-functions/organization /our-insights/why-diversity-matters.

19. Margaret Wheatley, "It's an Interconnected World," *Shambhala Sun*, April 2002, http://margaretwheatley.com/articles/interconnected.html.

20. www.thegreatbritishdiversityexperiment.com/.

21. https://implicit.harvard.edu/implicit/takeatest.html.

22. Emily Goldhill, "Empathy at Livity's," working paper, Livity's, January 2018.

12. The Call

1. Margaret J. Wheatley, *Turning to One Another: Simple Conversations to Restore Hope to the Future*, Berrett-Koehler, 2002, p. 13.

2. C. S. Lewis, *Mere Christianity* (1952); repr., Collins, 2012, p. 132.

ABOUT THE AUTHOR

Sam Conniff Allende is a multi-award-winning social entrepreneur and cofounder and former CEO of Livity, Don't Panic, and *Live* magazine. Since starting his entrepreneurial career at age nineteen, Conniff Allende has mentored thousands of talented young entrepreneurs and hustlers around the world.

Sam is an acclaimed public speaker, an advocate of "business as unusual" or corporate responsibility and accountability, and a purpose-driven strategy consultant to brands such as Red Bull, Unilever, and PlayStation.

Sam has refined the concepts explored in *Be More Pirate* by delivering workshops to senior executives in the headquarters of Google and Facebook, and also to hundreds of socially conscious entrepreneurs and innovators in the townships of South Africa, the heart of Baltimore, the center of Athens, and of course London, his hometown.